ASSESSING
ADULT LEARNING

The Professional Practices in Adult Education and Human Resource Development Series explores issues and concerns of practitioners who work in the broad range of settings in adult and continuing education and human resource development.

The books are intended to provide information and strategies on how to make practice more effective for professionals and those they serve. They are written from a practical viewpoint and provide a forum for instructors, administrators, policy makers, counselors, trainers, managers, program and organizational developers, instructional designers, and other related professionals.

Editorial correspondence should be sent to the Editor-in-Chief:

Michael W. Galbraith
Florida Atlantic University
Department of Educational Leadership
College of Education
Boca Raton, FL 33431

ASSESSING ADULT LEARNING

A Guide for Practitioners

Joseph J. Moran

KRIEGER PUBLISHING COMPANY
MALABAR, FLORIDA
2001

Original Edition   1997
Revised Edition   2001

Printed and Published by
KRIEGER PUBLISHING COMPANY
KRIEGER DRIVE
MALABAR, FLORIDA 32950

Library of Congress Cataloging-in-Publication Data

Moran, Joseph J.
    Assessing adult learning : a guide for practitioners / Joseph J.
Moran. — Rev. ed.
        p.   cm. — (Professional practices in adult education and
human resource development series)
    Includes bibliographical references and index.
    ISBN 1-57524-195-1 (alk. paper)
    1. Examinations   2. Examinations—Design.   3. Adult learning.
I. Title. II. Series.
LC5225.A75 M67   2001
374'.126—dc21   2001029616

10   9   8   7   6   5   4   3   2

This book is dedicated
to my wife Barbara.

CONTENTS

PREFACE

This updated edition is most notable for the topics that have been added or expanded. It retains the underlying organization as well as the two major goals of the original edition. The first of those goals is to help educators of adults become proficient in assessing learning. The second is to enable educators to use assessment procedures to improve the learning of those they serve.

It is important to stress that the focus of this edition remains on informal assessment. It is equally important to recognize that the term informal assessment does not refer to lackadaisical assessment. It refers to practices that are carefully devised and conducted by educators in collaboration with learners. It is informal because it does not rely on published materials and standardized procedures for administering, scoring, and interpreting tests. It depends on the creativity of educators to develop assessment materials and the judgment of educators to interpret assessment results and find ways to improve learning.

The first chapter provides a background in the basic principles of informal assessment. It stresses the importance of assessing the effectiveness of learning activities, the study skills of the learners, and the achievements of the learners. It elaborates on the role of assessment as a feedback mechanism in providing suggestions for improving learning. It also begins to develop one of the broader themes of the book—involving adult learners in planning the assessment of their learning.

Chapters 2 through 6 explain the strategies and tactics of informal assessment. Chapter 2 introduces the use of planning grids and concentrates on using them to assess instructional activities. It describes a series of practical techniques for gathering data from learners about their instructional activities in order to make immediate improvements for the learners.

Chapter 3 describes the uses for traditional paper and pencil tests in assessing individual achievement. It illustrates the principles for planning tests and writing objective and essay questions. It emphasizes the uses of assessment to promote higher order thinking such as analysis and synthesis. Chapter 4 explains scoring tests and interpreting test results. It includes a new section dealing with learners grading other learners, and it concludes with a discussion of the limitations of paper and pencil testing.

Chapter 5 addresses performance assessments and highlights the complementary roles of traditional testing and performance assessments. The chapter recommends using performance assessments of complex real-life tasks whenever such assessments are feasible because they accommodate the diverse learning styles of adults, encourage creativity, and help learners assess their own learning. Chapter 6 details procedures for collecting materials in portfolios in order to display the progress of individual learners toward their chosen goals. A new section outlines the possibilities for using the portfolios as a means of evaluating learning programs. Considerable attention is given to the use of conferences in portfolio assessments as a means of promoting collaboration between educators and adult learners as well as promoting the habit of lifelong learning.

Chapter 7 illustrates how the strategies and tactics of informal assessment can be applied in selected adult learning settings, including adult basic education, community education, and higher education. The chapter contains a significantly expanded section on assessing and grading learning that takes place in cooperative group activities. It also contains a new section on helping learners to assess their achievement in self-directed learning activities.

Chapter 8 considers how the principles of informal assessment pertain to several issues that cut across all areas of adult education. Included among the issues are multiculturalism, professional growth, and ethical practice in adult education. There is a new section on using assessment information to write responsible letters of reference for learners.

Just as in the original edition, a balance has been sought between explaining the principles of informal assessment as they appear in the professional literature and illustrating the practical applications of those principles. The result is a book written for people who are either practicing adult educators, supervising adult educators, or actively preparing to become adult educators. It is particularly suitable as a textbook in graduate courses on assessing learning. With its emphasis on involving learners in assessing their own learning, using assessment to focus learners on the higher mental processes, and promoting lifelong learning, it is also appropriate for a general course on adult learning. Since it has been written with relatively discrete chapters, the book is useful as a reference text for practicing adult educators who have a foundation in assessment.

Even though some topics have been expanded and others added to this edition, several topics often found in general purpose books on educational assessment are not addressed. This book does not cover commercially published tests or the educational statistics necessary to understand the use of such tests. Similarly, it leaves out the assessment of constructs such as intelligence and learning disabilities. It is hoped that omitting these topics, important as they are in some settings, has resulted in a book that readily enables adult educators to conduct informal assessment in ways that significantly improve the learning of their clients.

ACKNOWLEDGMENTS

I wish to thank my colleague of many years, Donald E. Carter, and series editor, Michael W. Galbraith, for reading drafts of this book and suggesting numerous improvements.

THE AUTHOR

Joseph J. Moran is Professor of Educational Foundations and Coordinator of the Master of Science Degree in Adult Education at State University College at Buffalo. He holds a Ph.D. in psychology from Emory University, an M.A. in education from Trinity College in Hartford, Connecticut, and a B.A. in psychology from Amherst College.

His research and teaching are focused on educational assessment, learning, and development. Besides his work in higher education, he has experience as an adult educator in literacy programs, secondary school diploma programs, workplace settings, and correction facilities. In addition, he is a licensed psychologist who has consulted in schools and community mental health centers regarding problems of learning and development.

He is the author of *Collaborative Professional Development for Teachers of Adults* (2001), which is also in the Professional Practices in Adult Education and Human Resource Development Series.

CHAPTER 1

Understanding the Basic Principles of Informal Assessment

Adult educators have one good reason to refine their skills for assessing learning informally and that is to improve learning. Here are three examples of how assessment exerts its influence: First, learning contracts, which are sometimes thought to embody what is distinctive about adult education, place marked emphasis on assessment. Even a glance at the sample contracts in Knowles's (1986) book, *Using Learning Contracts*, reveals the importance of assessment to the success of the contract. As part of the contracts, learners specify goals and the products that will serve as evidence that they reached those goals. Depending on their areas of study, they might specify a sellable watercolor, a reconditioned automobile engine that gets 30 miles per gallon, or a publishable 30-page manuscript. Throughout the contract the learners assess their progress. If progress is unsatisfactory they might increase their time spent on the contract, or alter their learning activities. When the learners determine that they have produced the specified products, they submit their work for assessment by one or more experts. Second, Gronlund and Linn (1990) reviewed a body of research and found that students, including adult students, who take courses on a pass/fail basis study less and learn less than when they submit themselves to the normal grading processes. Third, Foos and Fisher (1988) found that assessment practices significantly influence learning behaviors. Objective questions about factual material cause learners to limit themselves to memorizing information, but questions that ask learners to make inferences motivate them to analyze their material critically.

Even described as briefly as they are, these three observations reveal that assessing learning properly will help learners focus on important learning outcomes, study effectively, and learn material in meaningful ways. Equally, they imply that inadequate and/or inappropriate assessment will contribute to ineffective learning.

VARIETIES OF INFORMAL ASSESSMENT

The term *informal assessment* is not intended to connote anything that is unplanned, spur of the moment, or casual. It refers to assessment that is conducted by an educator with assessment instruments developed by the educator for the specific purpose of facilitating learning. It is informal in the sense that it does not involve standardized published procedures for administering, scoring, and interpreting tests. It depends for its success on educators constantly exercising professional judgment that is informed by an extensive array of principles and procedures. This book attempts to describe those principles and procedures in detail so that educators will be prepared to apply them in their individual situations.

Given the diversity of informal assessment, it is useful to group the procedures on the basis of the different functions they serve. Five varieties of informal assessment are discussed below.

Assessing Achievements of Individual Learners

One of the most traditional uses of informal assessment is assessing the achievements of individual learners. Examples of this process are

- a workshop leader administering a pretest to determine what participants know about the workshop topic before the learning activities begin
- an instructor calling on students in an introductory foreign language class to answer questions in the foreign language

- a trainer administering a test to determine what percentage of learners have achieved minimal competence in completing company forms.

Informal assessment is not restricted to assessing the achievements of individual learners as depicted in these examples.

Assessing Learning Activities

Informal assessment also includes a wide array of techniques designed to measure the effectiveness of particular learning activities as they have been implemented by an educator. Questions that might be asked about learning activities include Was the new demonstration helpful or confusing? Did a particular brainstorming session promote group cohesiveness?

Assessing Learning Behaviors

Perhaps one of the more overlooked and more intriguing aspects of informal assessment is assessing learner behaviors. Assessments of this type are concerned with questions like: Are the learners using appropriate study skills on their independent learning activities? Are they employing successful problem-solving strategies?

Learner Directed Assessment

It is easy to think of assessing learning as a top-down activity with a teacher at the top assessing the performance, even the worth, of students. In fact, what has been written in this chapter might even have strengthened that view. However, one of the important goals of this book is to prepare learners to become proficient in assessing their own learning achievements, activities, and behaviors.

The importance of being able to assess one's own learning

in both formal and informal educational settings has been emphasized by Stiggins (1994). He argues that unless learners can judge whether or not their performance is good or bad and make corrections when necessary, it can hardly be thought that their learning is satisfactory. Therefore, every effort should be made to structure assessment activities so they train learners to assess their learning.

The No-Assessment Option

Despite the many reasons for incorporating assessment into learning programs, there are educators who eschew assessment activities. Often they view assessment as punitive. Therefore, they recognize a role for evaluation in programs that profess to develop and/or certify the competence in learners, but they object to assessment activities when learners are pursuing personal goals. A group of professionals engaged in a study-abroad summer program would be an example of the latter situation. Another might be a group on a guided bird-watching hike. Would assessment really be helpful in these cases? Might it even be harmful?

No doubt, assessment that is poorly conceived can be destructive in any learning situation, including these. But well-planned assessment can also be quite helpful. For example, if the travelers were to plan before the start of a trip to convene at the end to report what they had learned, what meaning their learning had for them, and how they hoped to continue their learning, their experience could be enriched. Throughout the trip, the learners would continually relate their learning to their lives and recognize significance in events mentioned by other learners. In addition, the leader would learn what makes for successful study-abroad programs. If the bird-watchers were told ahead of time that they would be asked to answer some questions about what birds had been identified, by what markings, and in what terrain, the leader could get feedback on how effective his or her explanations had been, and the learners would have a second chance to store some of the very information they wanted to acquire.

A major premise of this book is that assessment suited to the learning situation is always helpful. In a sense, the remainder of the book is an attempt to explain how to match learning situations with helpful assessment.

RELATIONSHIP BETWEEN LEARNING AND ASSESSMENT ACTIVITIES

Informal assessment contributes to improved learning by providing information about how learning is proceeding. It is a feedback mechanism that enables educators and learners to make whatever adjustments might be needed in a learning program. For example, if a group of employees were being trained to use a word processing program, informal assessment in the form of a homework assignment after the first day of training would provide learners with an opportunity to consolidate what they had studied and determine whether or not they had focused on the important points in the presentation. It would also be an opportunity to identify topics that had not been mastered in order to provide more effective learning activities to target those topics. Such corrective measures, especially when they come early on, can make the difference between a successful and unsuccessful program.

Not to be overlooked is the likely occurrence that learners will demonstrate progress on the assessment. Such success motivates learners to persevere in demanding learning programs.

SEQUENCING LEARNING AND ASSESSMENT ACTIVITIES

In order for assessment to benefit learning, activities must be properly sequenced. The usual sequence of learning and assessment activities in a learning program is depicted in Figure 1.1 and described below. The sequence reveals that there are multiple types of assessment that come at several points in a learning program. In addition, it highlights the ways assessment

1. Set Learning Goals.
2. Select Learning and Assessment Activities.
3. Initiate Learning Activities.
4. Assess and Adjust Learning Activities.
5. Assess and Adjust Learning Behaviors.
6. Assess Achievement and Remediate As Needed.
7. Complete Learning Activities.
8. Assess Final Learning Achievement.
9. Identify Effective Learning Activities for Future Use.

Figure 1.1 The Sequence of Learning and Assessment Activities

information is immediately analyzed for indications of how learning can be enhanced.

Set Learning Goals

It may seem obvious that the first step in planning a learning program is to set the learning goals. Unfortunately, educators sometimes set them only implicitly. The key is to write them down so they can give direction to all the planning that follows. Three procedures that commonly help in setting goals are

1. asking learners what they want to learn
2. testing their competence on goals specified by authorities such as employers and other educators
3. reviewing the learning goals of similar groups.

Select Learning and Assessment Activities

The second step may appear as though it should be divided in two—select learning activities and select assessment activities. But they are combined here to stress the point that learning activities and assessment activities should be planned in coordination with each other. Consider this somewhat simplified example: An educator is planning learning activities for a workshop on mandatory reporting of child abuse by professionals. Participants must demonstrate competence in order to have their licenses renewed. The learning goals are to know when and how to report. What should the learning activities be? Deciding how to measure what the participants will do to demonstrate their competence will help in choosing the learning activities. If participants are going to take a multiple-choice test with 10% of the questions on definitions of terms, 20% on reporting procedures, and 70% on deciding whether or not to report specific simulated situations, then learning activities are best chosen with these proportions in mind. Approximately one-third of the time would be given to distributing information about definitions and procedures. A multimedia lecture presentation with handouts would be effective. The remaining time would be given to making and evaluating decisions to report or not report specific situations. Demonstrations, small group discussions, and role-playing decision making might be appropriate. Coordinating learning and assessment activities helps learners reach goals and perform well on the test.

Initiate Learning Activities

The third step is to begin the planned activities. Clearly an important step, it is mentioned here only briefly in order to keep the focus on assessment. The key point is that assessment is conducted on multiple occasions in the midst of the learning program, and each time adjustments may be made on the basis of the information for the remainder of the program.

Assess and Adjust Learning Activities

The fourth step is assessing learning activities. As the first assessment, it emphasizes that the primary role of assessment is to improve learning. It also indicates that informal assessment encompasses many techniques in addition to the familiar objective and essay tests. Two examples of assessing learning activities are (1) ending a presentation by asking each learner to write a description of the most confusing point in a presentation and (2) interviewing a group halfway through their learning program about what they would like changed in the program. As these examples imply, assessing learning activities is intended to be used to make immediate improvements in ongoing learning activities. There should be no waiting to plan how the educator might do better with the next group of learners.

Assess and Adjust Learning Behaviors

The fifth step is to assess learning behaviors. It seems to be the step most frequently neglected at all levels of education. Even in settings where it might be reasonable to think that adult learners need training in appropriate learning behaviors—for example, adult literacy or retraining programs—it is rare for educators to examine the learning behaviors of the learners. Conversely, in settings where it might be reasonable to expect that the learners have mastered learning skills, individual learners might engage in a number of self-defeating learning behaviors.

Fortunately, assessing learning behaviors is relatively straightforward. It might entail simply asking learners to record their thoughts as they solve an assigned problem or the procedures they follow in reading a textbook. Their reports can yield valuable indications of glitches that can be rectified. There is a bonus to this process; the customized feedback that the learners receive demonstrates that their learning is important to their educators.

Assess Achievement and Remediate As Needed

The sixth step begins with assessments of what learners have achieved in terms of the stated goals. Simply asking questions and having volunteers give answers orally is a way of gathering information about the learners' progress. Of course, it is somewhat unreliable because it does not gather information from all the learners. Quizzes, independent assignments (homework), and individual conferences all provide high-quality information about the progress of individual learners. When progress is lagging, it is possible to intervene by reviewing material, adjusting workloads, teaching study skills, and so forth. Interventions can be directed at individuals or the group of learners as a whole.

Complete Learning Activities

Completing the learning activities is the seventh step. It is not a subject for elaboration here except to note that these activities are not always completed as initially planned, but are continually adjusted by the results of the assessments of learning activities, behaviors, and achievements.

Assess Final Learning Achievement

Final assessment of learning achievement is the eighth step. Often it is a traditional classroom test constructed of multiple-choice items and essay questions. However, different types of assessments are possible and many times preferable. Although grading is not necessary, it is important that, as part of the final assessment, learners receive both feedback about their accomplishments and support to continue with their learning.

Identify Effective Learning Activities for Future Use

The ninth and last step emphasizes using assessment to improve learning. All information and especially the final assessments of the learners' achievements constitute the feedback for judging the effectiveness of the learning activities. In areas where learners rated activities favorably and performed well, the associated learning activities can be judged successful. Where learners did not rate activities favorably or did not perform well, the activities should be revised.

This sequence can be adapted to apply to short learning programs such as one-day workshops, long programs such as college courses, and to units within a long program such as a unit on discipline in a program on parenting. The important point is not so much to observe the sequence but to coordinate activities so that assessment information can be used to improve learning both immediately and in the future.

BASIC ASSESSMENT TERMS

In order to fully discuss the potential of assessment as a feedback mechanism to enhance adult learning, it is necessary to have a vocabulary for describing assessment practices. The core of the assessment vocabulary is introduced below.

Educational Tests

An educational test is any instrument or procedure designed to determine what a person has learned. It could be a set of questions the learner is to answer with paper and pencil. It could be a set of job-related tasks the learner is to perform while being observed. The key point is that a test should be sufficiently systematic so that it can be used with different learners and yield comparable information about each learner.

Educational Measurement

Educational measurement is the use of tests to describe quantitatively what persons have learned, and what they have not learned.

Evaluation and Assessment

Evaluation and assessment are such closely related terms that in everyday conversation, they might be used interchangeably. For the purposes of this book, evaluation refers to using measurements to reach a judgment regarding how well a person or group of persons has achieved learning goals. Evaluation is not a priority in this book because it is not routinely appropriate for adult education. It is discussed only in regard to specific situations such as grading.

Assessment refers to using measurements to describe a learner's achievement and to make recommendations for additional learning activities. Whereas evaluation is normally carried out by an authority who is in effect handing down a judgment on one or more learners, assessment is normally accomplished cooperatively by educators and learners. As implied in the title of this book, the emphasis here is on assessment—using tests to characterize a learner's achievement in order to select learning activities and learning behaviors to facilitate his or her future learning.

BASIC ASSESSMENT OBJECTIVES

Assessment is more likely to be successful when it is conducted for a clearly stated purpose. There are two considerations that distinguish purposes for assessing learning.

Formative and Summative Assessment

The first of these considerations has already been mentioned, but only implicitly. It pertains to when measurements are made and how they are acted upon. Formative assessment refers to measurements and conclusions that are made during the course of a learning program. It is intended to determine whether or not an existing learning program is functioning satisfactorily or should be modified before it is completed. Formative assessment tends to be brief and consists of multiple assessments of the individual portions of a learning program. An ungraded pop quiz to get an idea of how learners are doing after the second learning session in a five-session program is an example of formative assessment. The educator might use the results to modify the learning activities and the learners might use the results to adjust their learning behaviors.

Summative assessment refers to measurements made at the end of a learning unit or learning program. They result in final judgments about the achievement of learners and the effectiveness of learning activities. An example of a summative assessment is a final examination in a graduate course on adult development. Grades will be assigned in large part on the basis of the test. The educator and learners may make modifications based on the results but the modifications will be for a different course.

The bar exam for law school graduates is another example of a summative evaluation at the end of a learning program. It is a single extensive examination that yields judgment about whether or not each of those tested is fit to practice law in a particular state. The percentage of graduates from each school passing is taken as an indication of the quality of the program at the individual schools and low passing rates may lead to changing or even terminating programs.

Educators are encouraged to plan both formative and summative assessments. As the examples are meant to imply, different techniques should be used for each.

Criterion-, Norm-, and Self-Referenced Interpretations

The second consideration pertains to the standards that are used in making interpretations of the measurements. Criterion-referenced assessments are intended to determine whether or not a learner has achieved an objectively set level of competence. In a sense, they are the preferred method.

A criterion-referenced evaluation might be required for a person studying to become an emergency medical technician

(EMT). The test would be composed of questions that experts agree every EMT should be able to answer correctly. A significant portion of the evaluation would be actual or simulated performance of emergency medical procedures designated by experts. The criterion is the level of performance that is set and accepted by experts, normally 85 to 90% correct. It is seen that for criterion-referenced assessments the content of the test, the difficulty of the test, and the type of items on the test are determined by the objective demands of the learning goals.

Norm-referenced assessments are usually selected when learners are studying material for which there is no agreement on what a person must know. A course in English literature would be an example; there would be some but not great agreement on which or how many writers a person needed to study or how well a person needed to analyze a poem to earn a passing grade. In these situations, assessments are based on how well a learner has mastered the material compared to the other learners in the class and how well the learner did compared to the norm for the class.

Self-referenced assessments are used when the learning goals are personal. For example, if learners were involved in religious education for their private spiritual development there would be no need for or way of estimating what the learners must or should know at the end of the program. Nor would there be any need to compare one learner to another. The appropriate indicator of success is the learners own opinion. Similarly, if learners were enrolled in an informal creative writing course, collecting and presenting their writing to display their versatility would be helpful to them in planning what they might try next, but trying to impose objective standards or making comparisons to other writers would be inappropriate.

The distinctions among types of interpretations guide educators in two important ways. First, deciding how measurements will be interpreted helps in designing appropriate tests. If learners are to be assessed against objective standards, as in criterion-referenced assessment, then the educator should procure information about such standards and develop precise test questions or tasks no more difficult than necessary to measure their attainment. Both formative and summative measures should follow this model. For norm-referenced assessment, test questions and tasks should vary from objective to subjective, from easy to difficult, and from simple memory work to critical and creative thought. When learners engage in self-assessment, they should obviously take part in designing the assessment. Their participation should include taking time within the learning program to develop a set of learning goals and standards for when they have achieved those goals. Rarely will they want to give themselves a test. They might choose a group discussion where they share what they learned about their subject matter and how they have applied their learning to their lives. They might elect to write statements of what they learned and what they plan to study next.

Second, after educators have selected standards and designed their assessments, and before beginning learning activities, they should inform the learners about how they will be assessed. Such early information enables learners to match their learning behaviors to the assessment (Foos & Fisher, 1988). If the assessment has been matched to the learning goals of the program, learning will be facilitated.

ASSESSMENT PRINCIPLES

Assessments are based on evidence gathered from tests. Therefore, multiple high-quality instruments must be chosen for their suitability to the learning goals and the characteristics of the learners.

Use High-Quality Instruments

There are four characteristics that help educators judge the quality of an instrument: objectivity, reliability, validity, and adequacy. Many books provide comprehensive technical explanations of these terms. However, within this book they are described simply as they relate to informal assessment.

Objectivity

An instrument is objective if different people would score the answers for the same person on the same test in the same way. Therefore, a spelling test, a multiple-choice test, and a count of words typed correctly and incorrectly within a 10-minute period are among the most objective tests. Ratings of performances such as cursive handwriting can be made relatively objective by training raters and providing samples of cursive at several levels of proficiency.

Reliability

Reliability refers to whether or not an instrument would yield essentially the same scores if it were used two or more times with the same learners. From the standpoint of informal assessment, it is not often possible or advisable to go through the large amount of work required to assess the reliability of an instrument statistically. But it is relatively easy to take precautions to ensure satisfactory reliability in assessment. Whenever possible use instruments that are objective. Sometimes it is not appropriate to use tests that are objective. An example is when learners are demonstrating artistic accomplishments. In such cases have two or more raters judge the achievement of the learning outcomes. It is often advisable for each rater to give separate ratings for multiple criteria. This is the procedure used for scoring figure skating contests where a panel of raters each assign skaters scores for technical expertise and for artistic expression.

Validity

Validity refers to whether or not a test measures what it claims to measure in the situation in which it is used. For example, an apparently sound multiple-choice test that was written at the ninth-grade reading level, but was given to learners who read at the sixth-grade level, would not be valid for those learners. Similarly a test that includes material not actually covered in the learning program would not be valid even though the material was important and should have been covered. There are several planning procedures that go a long way toward ensuring that the use of a given informal assessment instrument will be valid. These procedures are detailed in Chapter 3.

Adequacy

Adequacy refers to whether or not a test measures all of the learning outcomes that learners were trying to achieve within a unit of study. For example, if a test of U.S. history from the first colony to the present contained only questions about prerevolutionary dates, it would not be considered adequate for several reasons. First, it failed to cover the period after 1775, and second, it failed to measure any of the more sophisticated ways of knowing American history such as thinking critically about historical controversies.

Use Multiple Instruments

It is important to use high-quality assessment instruments, but it is equally important to keep in mind that one instrument is rarely capable of providing all the information that will be needed to make a significant educational decision. Just as an essay test will not be able to measure all a person has learned about a topic, an inspection of a chair built by a learner will not adequately indicate all of the learner's carpentry skills, and one observation will not reveal all about an educator's skill in delivering a lecture. In general, assessments are best when they are based on two or more measurements taken with two or more instruments. And in particular, decisions about an individual should not be based on a single test score or observation.

Use Authentic Instruments

Just as important as selecting an array of high quality instruments is selecting the most authentic instruments possible.

The general rule is to select tests composed of tasks that closely approximate the tasks learners attempt or will attempt in their lives outside the learning program. Therefore, playing the scale is preferable to writing the notes; dissecting a worm is preferable to drawing its intestines; and printing a table with a computer graphics package is superior to describing the "print" command.

Accommodate to Learner Characteristics

Even authentic, technically sound assessment instruments may prove ineffective at improving learning, unless they are accepted if not actually embraced by the learners. As most educators know, learners have widely divergent but strongly held views about what constitutes acceptable and desirable assessment. Their views reflect their personal characteristics, of which they are often only vaguely aware. Therefore, it behooves the professional educator to find a way to take those characteristics into account.

An excellent guide to accommodating the characteristics of learners is found in a model of learning styles developed by Grow (1991). According to his model, learners progress through the following stages: dependent, interested, involved, and self-directed. Grow has described what he thought learners at different stages would prefer by way of learning activities. By integrating those descriptions with information regarding adult cognitive development (Moran, 1991), it is possible to infer what assessment activities would be successful with different types of learners.

Dependent Learners

Dependent learners value authority and acquiring objective information. They think of knowledge as made up of facts that have been proven true. They prefer a top-down assessment system exemplified by drill and recitation for formative assessment and objective tests and performance observations for summative assessment. They would probably see criterion-referenced assessments as the most legitimate assessments.

Interested Learners

Interested learners find inspiration in their teachers and apparently in the prospects of learning what new ideas might be proved right and what old ideas might be proved wrong. Socratic discussions provide them with congenial formative evaluation. They probably prefer a mix of objective and essay tests frequently found in college freshman and sophomore courses for summative assessments.

Involved Learners

Involved learners wish to take some control of their learning. They seem to enjoy generating and testing ideas of their own. For formative assessment, they would see merit in rating their performances in their preferred learning activities which are seminars. For summative assessment, they would lean toward term papers, community service and other group projects. Because they seem to think of knowledge as being relative rather than absolute, they are likely to be more comfortable with norm-referenced than with criterion-referenced assessments.

Self-directed Learners

Self-directed learners are sophisticated learners who are often capable of postformal thought (Moran, 1991) which is defined as thinking across theoretical systems, integrating feelings with thoughts, accepting contradiction in what is known, and addressing problems for which there are no single final solutions. According to Grow (1991), they prefer learning contracts where they can choose both the learning and the assessment activities. They want feedback on how successfully they have integrated alternative perspectives into their work. Since they see educators as colleagues rather than as authorities, their preference is for self-referenced assessments and/or critiques from two or more peers at both the formative and summative levels.

The importance of matching assessment activities to learner characteristics is evident in the two possible mismatches described below: The best constructed multiple-choice tests are going to offend self-directed learners who will feel demeaned by what they consider the demands to "regurgitate" what they have studied. They will feel cheated of opportunities for critical thinking and making applications of what they learned to their individual lives. Similarly, learning contracts are going to fail with dependent learners. Dependent learners will be confused and express their confusion in the form of complaints that they "don't know what you want." They will have a sense of not having learned anything. In either case, the learners will chafe and possibly withdraw their energy, if not their actual bodies, in revolt against the mismatch with their styles.

This section on accommodating learner characteristics would not be complete without mentioning three additional points. The first is that assessing adult learning is not a matter of applying the assessment procedures that work with children to the content that adults might be learning. The procedures that work with children are sometimes appropriate for dependent learners. However, for more sophisticated learners, it is important to use procedures that are matched to their capabilities. Second, assessing adult learning is a matter of developing and using techniques that not only match the learner's preferred style but challenge the learners to move to higher levels. For example, it would seem inappropriate to always assess dependent concrete learners with objective tests of memory for information. The assessment would have the effect of limiting their growth. It would be important to challenge them with more advanced forms of first formative and then summative assessments. Third, within any group of learners, there will be people at various stages in Grow's model. (This is so, in part, because people develop from dependent to self-directed one content area at a time. Someone might be self-directed in his or her area of expertise, but dependent or interested in a new area of study.) No one assessment mode will accommodate all of them so an educator is likely to be most successful when blending in all levels of assessment while patiently shifting to the most advanced forms.

WHAT IS NEXT?

Having reviewed the basic concepts and principles of assessment, our next step is to look at how they are put into practice. Chapter 2 provides an examination of formative assessment of learning activities, behaviors, and progress in adult education.

CHAPTER 2

Assessing the Learning Process

Assessing the learning process is one of the more intriguing and one of the more neglected aspects of informal assessment. The goal is to identify which aspects of a learning program are promoting and which are inhibiting learning. Assessments of the learning process are formative rather than summative so they are conducted early and frequently during a learning program. The results are used to make immediate adjustments in the program. They usually take 5 to 10 minutes for a group of learners to complete, and an additional 20 to 30 minutes for an educator to interpret. Sometimes their greatest benefit is the sense of empowerment that learners experience as a result of having their assessment input form the basis for improvements in their ongoing learning programs.

STRUCTURING ASSESSMENTS

All informal assessment, including assessment of the learning process, is conducted in terms of progress toward stated goals. Angelo and Cross (1993) have revealed that in adult education there are so many goals, both implicit and explicit, that important ones may be easily overlooked. In addition, they have provided the basis for a system to enable educators to assess progress toward a variety of goals in an orderly and comprehensive fashion. The system is based on a set of six categories of educational goals.

Educational Goals

The six categories of goals Angelo and Cross (1993) listed are Thinking Skills, Basic Academic Skills, Discipline-Specific Knowledge and Skills, Liberal Arts Values, Work Preparation, and Personal Development. Since they are general, they are approached differently in various settings, but they are all applicable in virtually every adult education program. The following are examples of what constitutes each category of goals.

Thinking Skills

Thinking skills refer to facility in distinguishing fact from opinion, identifying stated and unstated assumptions, detecting errors in logic, synthesizing ideas, recognizing the limitations of human knowledge, creating, and using the scientific method.

Basic Academic Skills

Basic academic skills are competencies in note taking, textbook reading, test taking, written composition, numerical computation, public speaking, memorizing, and computer literacy.

Discipline-Specific Knowledge and Skills

Discipline-specific knowledge and skills vary according to discipline. Examples from history are knowing dates and applying principles of historiography. Examples from word processing are keyboarding and managing files.

Liberal Arts Values

Liberal arts values are abstractions that are observed as openness to new ideas, appreciation of other cultures, dedication to lifelong learning, and commitment to civic responsibility.

Work Preparation

Work preparation includes understanding the skills required in different occupations and the personality types associated with success in different occupations. It also entails appreciation of the importance of work habits, leadership skills, working collaboratively, and following directions. In addition, it includes commitment to achievement and ethical behavior in the workplace.

Personal Development

Personal development refers to self-esteem, commitment to exploring and enacting one's values, pursuit of wellness, commitment to moral behavior, and maintaining relationships.

By themselves these categories of goals can aid educators in choosing important learning outcomes. But they become especially useful for planning formative assessments when they are placed in a planning grid.

The Planning Grid

The planning grid for formative assessment is constructed by placing the categories of educational goals in the left hand margin. The top margin of the grid consists of the three aspects of the learning process that were mentioned in Chapter 1, and are reviewed briefly below:

Learning Activities

Learning activities are structured events such as lectures, demonstrations, debates, discussions, problem-solving sessions, field trips, and any similar events. Assessing learning activities enables a facilitator to decide whether to continue or to modify the types of activities that learners have been engaged in.

Learning Behaviors

Learning behaviors are the individual actions of learners. They include not only whether a learner reads a book, but how that learner reads the book. The educator might want to know if the learner read it on time; at a reasonable time of day; used the appropriate reading strategies; and took detailed notes. Particularly for adults whose learning history is not marked by success, assessing learning behaviors can point toward improved performance.

Learning Progress

Learning progress refers to whether or not learners are in fact mastering the material they are trying to learn. Assessment of learning progress may take the form of a quiz to determine how many learners know the definitions and how many can solve sample problems. It enables facilitators and learners to know if some material should be reviewed by individuals or groups of learners, if learning activities can be made more challenging, or if they are appropriate as designed and implemented.

A copy of the planning grid is in Figure 2.1. The dates in the body of the table can be ignored for the moment. They illustrate one of the steps in the planning process which is described below.

Using the Planning Grid

The grid is normally most useful for planning that takes place prior to the beginning of the learning program, when the educator asks, "What kinds of information can I get during the program that will help me keep the program running smoothly right up to the end?" Answers will probably be based on personal experience. For example, an educator might recall that the performance of a previous group of low-literacy learners had been uneven—sometimes quite good and other times disappointing. Therefore, it is appropriate to assess the basic aca-

	Learning Activities	Learning Behavior	Learning Progress
I. Thinking Skills			
II. Basic Academic Skills		Oct. 10	
III. Discipline-Specific Knowledge and Skills			Nov. 15
IV. Liberal Arts Values	Feb. 20		
V. Work Preparation			
VI. Personal Development			

Complete by writing in the date and the Classroom Assessment Technique(s) to be used. Consult Angelo and Cross (1993) for examples of Classroom Assessment Techniques.

Figure 2.1 Planning Grid for Assessing the Learning Process

demic skills of the incoming group to see if breakdowns in basic skills might be contributing to the expected ups and downs in performance. After looking at the grid, the educator decides to assess behaviors, specifically how learners outline their written material. The assessment is planned for the week prior to the due date of October 17 for a major writing assignment. Therefore, Oct. 10 is written in the cell on the grid under Learning Behaviors and across from Basic Academic Skills.

A second answer to the opening questions might be, "I will need to know if the learners have comprehended the basic principles covered in the first unit." If that unit were to end on November 15th, an assessment of comprehension would be scheduled for that date as it has in Figure 2.1. Next, in order to improve the program, the educator would use the grid as a checklist to make sure that nothing important has been left off the roster. The educator might be prompted to inquire about the extent to which learners are acquiring liberal arts values—specifically, if they are opening up to new ideas. February 20 has been set aside for assessing the success of learning activities in promoting this value.

Since assessments of learning take away from the time and energy that needs to be shared with learning activities, the planning requires balancing the desire to gather all the useful information possible and the need to spend as little time as possible performing assessments. Similarly, interpreting assessment results and planning adjustments in learning activities takes away from the time and energy of the educator. Therefore, it is *not* recommended that an educator conduct an assessment for all or even a majority of the cells in the grid within any given learning program. For educators who are beginning to develop skill in assessing the learning process, it is wise to schedule no more than one or two per learning program.

SELECTING ASSESSMENT TECHNIQUES

Once the topics and dates for assessment have been determined, the next task is to select the appropriate techniques. In general effective techniques should be

- Brief
- Enjoyable
- Related to important issues for the learner
- Interpreted readily enough so that feedback can be given to the learners at the next group meeting

In addition, assessment techniques yield the most valid information when they record information from the largest possible percentage of learners within a given program. For this reason, there is a strong preference for collecting information in written form either as individual statements or as statements endorsed by the learners as representing a consensus among them.

A brief review of some established techniques follows. As will be seen, educators can readily become skillful at selecting, modifying, and/or devising effective techniques for assessing the learning process; nonetheless, readers are encouraged to refer to Angelo and Cross (1993) for a fuller account of these techniques and their use.

Assessing Learning Activities

There are two phases to assessing learning activities. One is preassessment, or gathering information to help plan suitable learning activities for a group that has not begun its program. The second is assessing the suitability of activities that have already been completed.

Preassessment

Dean (1994) has written a comprehensive description of the preassessment process. He noted the importance of consulting multiple sources of information for the preassessment. One source is an educator's prior experience with similar content and learners. A second is composed of published reports, and a third source is the experience of one's colleagues. A fourth could be a survey distributed to the learners prior to or at the initial meeting of the group.

In organizing the preassessment, an educator might begin by jotting down what is likely to be true of the yet-to-be-met learners for each of the six categories of educational goals. Then he or she would determine what additional questions relating to those goals should be asked of the learners. Finally, the educator would devise brief assessment procedures to get answers to those questions. Samples of items that might appear on a variety of preassessment surveys follow:

- Thinking Skills
  Please indicate which of the following are statements of fact or opinion
- Basic Academic Skills
  Describe the steps you follow when you read a chapter in a textbook.

- Discipline-Specific Knowledge and Skills
  What skills do you already have that are related to this learning program?
  Please solve the following algebra problems and show all your work.
- Liberal Arts Values
  What are you most interested in learning?
  List the books you have read simply for your enjoyment in the last 6 months.
- Work Preparation
  What would help you upgrade your work skills?
  Have you ever encountered an ethical dilemma on the job? Please explain.
- Personal Development
  Present a description of the stages in Grow's (1991) model of learner development and ask learners to choose the one that best describes themselves. For example, What do you hope to get out of this program; What personal and professional goals are you pursuing?

In some ways this process is simpler, with more sophisticated learners because they know about themselves as learners. Of course, the process is also simpler if the group is small. An educator who is faced with assessing less sophisticated learners, or larger groups is advised to consult the work of Dean (1994).

Mid-Program Assessment

Unlike preassessments, assessing learning activities in the midst of a learning program calls on the learners to make judgments of how well the program is going. Immediately following any activity, the educator asks the learners for their opinion of that activity. It is common for educators to ask about (1) clarity of presentations such as lectures, demonstrations, and simulations; (2) suitability of physical setting; (3) psychological atmosphere; and (4) learning materials such as overhead transparencies and videotapes.

Samples of questions associated with each educational goal are found below:

- Thinking Skills
What part of today's activities were the most thought provoking for you?
- Basic Academic Skills
How easily could you follow the organization and take notes on today's activities? What made it difficult to do so?
- Discipline-Specific Knowledge and Skills
Angelo and Cross (1993) reported that a teacher of writing skills asked learners to report the most helpful comments they received from their peers when they reviewed one another's writing in small groups. The comments were taken as an indication of the effectiveness of the small group activity.
- Liberal Arts Values
Did any part of today's activities make you want to go out and learn something on your own? If so, what?
- Work Preparation
What part of today's activities were most relevant to your work?
- Personal Development
What part of today's activities were most relevant to your personal life?

A Generic Technique

In practice, the form of mid-program assessments of learning activities need not vary much from one educational goal to another. Educators may find it more suitable to use Brookfield's (1990) Critical Incident technique as a means to assess all six levels of educational goals. It works by asking learners to write out answers to questions such as the following at the end of an activity:

- What most engaged you in learning today?
- What most distanced you from learning today?
- What was most helpful to you?

- What was most confusing to you?
- What was most enlightening for you?

Clearly, this set of questions or an altered version could be used after most learning sessions, especially the sessions that include a variety of learning activities. Because of their general nature, these questions give relatively more latitude to learners in deciding what to assess and, therefore, may tap their concerns more directly.

When the same general questions are used for multiple assessments, there are options for interpreting the results. On the one hand, the answers should be collected by the educator immediately to be examined for ideas about immediate changes in the learning program. They could be returned so learners can store their comments in journals to be examined at the end of the program for clues about their own characteristics as learners. Subsequently, the educator would also examine the journals for information about the changing, hopefully improving, effectiveness of the learning activities as the result of adjustments made during the program.

Assessing the Learning Activities Program

There is one strikingly effective method of evaluating all the learning activities in a program simultaneously. It is the Small Group Instructional Diagnosis (SGID) (Coffman, 1991; Diamond, 1988). The diagnosis begins with the educator asking the learners to brainstorm a list of the criteria that they use when they evaluate a learning program. The educator simply records their ideas on a chalk board. Often the list is condensed by combining criteria on the list. The criteria usually fall within the AAACE categories: Achievement, Activities, Atmosphere, Content, and Evaluation. If any of these areas is entirely unrepresented, the educator might ask if the learners would like to add it.

The educator leaves the room and learners form groups of approximately five in which they discuss the learning program in terms of one criterion at a time. Each group fills out the SGID form for each of the criteria. A copy of the form is in Figure 2.2. One of the learners collects the sheets and returns them to the educator. The educator reviews the sheets privately, and at the next group meeting holds a discussion with the class to clarify issues and possibly plan adjustments.

The SGID allows learners maximum freedom in choosing what to assess, but its main advantage is that the small group discussions elicit considerably more reflection on the part of the learners than do most requests for their opinions as individuals. The main disadvantage is that it gives the educator little input regarding what is assessed. It seems only natural then to schedule an SGID on the planning grid as a complement to the assessments the educator chooses to conduct.

A second advantage of the SGID method of assessing learning activities is the message it sends to adult learners. It says that their opinions are valued by the facilitator, and it says that the facilitator does not put himself or herself above the learners. Of course, the extent to which recommendations are implemented immediately in the learning program is the really crucial aspect of the assessment. When a facilitator makes a change that has been recommended by the learners, the learners recognize that they are not only held in esteem, but they are competent to direct their own learning. This is a major step in their development as self-directed lifelong learners.

A third advantage is the impact of the discussions on the views learners have of themselves. Learners are likely to think that all people learn as they do, and, as a result, fail to consider that there may be significant differences in learning styles. The discussions bring home the importance of these differences. For example, if a dependent learner complains that he would like more lectures and less discussions, an involved or self-directed learner might demur by saying that the discussions are the most worthwhile part of the activities because they generate lots of ideas from which a person can make up his or her own mind. The dependent learner might see the point and begin to look for and find the value in the discussions.

For all of its benefits, the SGID process is actually quite

Name of Learning Program   Date
Criterion Rating of the program on the criterion
Consensus of the group
Significant dissent from the consensus
Suggestions for change

Figure 2.2 Small Group Instructional Diagnosis Form

simple, empowering for the learners, and informative for the educator. Its advantages are maximized when it is used at the right time. Generally that right time is after the learners have coalesced as a social unit and before the learning program is half over. These conditions more or less ensure that the learners have had ample exposure to the learning activities in the program, that they will discuss them candidly, and that there will be sufficient time to make adjustments in the learning activities if that were to prove advisable.

ASSESSING LEARNING BEHAVIORS

The term *learning behaviors* refers to whatever learners do when they are consciously trying to learn material. Unfortunately, learners, and especially adult learners who have been away from organized learning programs for extended periods, engage in many ineffective and/or counterproductive learning behaviors. Therefore, assessing learning behaviors is not only appropriate but one of the surest ways to overcome learning difficulties experienced by individual learners. Examples of techniques for assessing learning behaviors have been arranged according to educational goals and are presented below:

Thinking Skills

Angelo and Cross (1993) have suggested a procedure for assessing how learners think about their own thinking. They ask learners to write a running account of what they do and say to themselves as they memorize material, solve problems, or engage in any other mental activity. It is somewhat time consuming to examine the running accounts, but the results are likely to be well worth the effort. For example, an educator could determine if learners are telling themselves to use mnemonics as does the learner who says, "I wonder if I can make a word out of the first letter in the names of the Great Lakes. Then I would only have to remember the word." Or an educator might find out if the learners attempt to direct their thinking as someone who is faced with writing a paper about health care might do in saying, "I might try outlining the advantages and disadvantages of each of these health care policies. Advantages and disadvantages usually help." This technique not only assesses important thinking skills, but it encourages learners to get in the habit of thinking about their thinking.

Basic Academic Skills

Academic skills should probably be assessed frequently with relatively unsophisticated learners. Often they can be assessed without loss of group learning time. For example, collecting notebooks is a good way to assess note-taking skills. Collecting the first drafts written in preparation for writing essay answers will reveal how many learners are even writing first drafts as well as the types of revisions they are making.

Discipline-Specific Knowledge and Skills

The behaviors associated with specific disciplines are particularly significant in areas that involve physical performances. From holding a brush in an art course, to sitting for a keyboarding exercise, to adjusting a microscope in a science laboratory, there is a tremendous range of behaviors that need to be assessed systematically. The key is to observe and record the performance of all the learners. Often all that is needed is a chart listing behaviors on one margin and learners' names along the other margin, with checks to indicate satisfactory behaviors.

Liberal Arts Values

Behaviors in the area of liberal arts are sometimes most useful as a means of inferring commitment to values. There are several such behaviors that educators can observe directly but unobtrusively. For example, an important liberal arts value is acceptance and celebration of cultural differences. An educator can assess the development of this value by noting whether learners form single ethnic or multiethnic groups. Some values would have to be assessed indirectly. For example, asking learners to describe ways in which they have applied what they learned in a program to understanding and/or helping their communities would give an indication of growth in civic responsibility.

Work Preparation

It seems certain that many learning behaviors that contribute to academic success also contribute to work preparation. Time management, punctuality, and, yes, neatness are important. Neglecting to note such behaviors as the foundation for successful learning may undermine work preparation because the neglect suggests they are not important. One recommendation is to request that all learners keep a diary of their work and leisure for 1 week at the beginning and 1 week at the end of the learning program. Conclude the assessment by having all learners compare their diaries for the 2 weeks and offer an assessment of the change in their time management skills and in their perseverance in their studies.

Personal Development

What learners say to themselves about their learning can have significant impact on their achievement. It makes sense then to assess whether they are encouraging or discouraging their development as learners by having them report their self-statements. This can be done with open-ended questions like, "Everybody talks to themselves about important matters. What do you say to yourself about yourself, about your plans to study, and about your expectations for success?" This type of assessment can be written or done in a questionnaire format as depicted in Figure 2.3. The questionnaire might be preferable for learners who are relatively less sophisticated and fearful of admitting to self-statements.

ASSESSING LEARNING PROGRESS

Assessing learning progress enables educators to make determinations such as what material should be reviewed, what individuals should get special attention, and when it is appropriate to begin new units of material.

Thinking Skills

Quite possibly the most widely used technique for assessing learning progress is asking questions orally. This is a simple and effective technique because it blends in with learning activities,

Use the scale to indicate how likely you are to make each of the following statements to yourself.

1	2	3	4	5
Very Unlikely	Somewhat Unlikely	Not Sure	Somewhat Likely	Very Likely

I am never going to learn this stuff. _____

Everything will be okay if I do my work on schedule. _____

Figure 2.3 Sample Form for Assessing Learner Self-Statements

requires relatively little time, and seems to add a conversational tone to learning activities. Many experts have recommended that educators carefully plan questions so that they cover thinking skills as well as knowledge of factual material. For example, in a training session on writing effective business letters, a factual question would be, "What are the parts of a business letter?" A question to assess thinking skills might be, "What is the main point in the sample letter? Was it thoroughly explained?" These questions involving thinking skills make learning activities challenging, and they remind learners to concentrate a portion of their attention on thinking skills.

Despite the advantages of oral questioning in assessing learning progress, it can be misleading because it rarely obtains information on all or even a majority of the learners in a group. After all, asking questions of every learner is terribly time consuming and likely to become boring, punitive, or both. As a result, the educator may learn what the most outspoken learners know, but be kept in the dark as far as the progress of the quiet, shy, and/or less knowledgeable learners. Therefore, oral questioning should be supplemented by techniques that gather information from all learners.

Angelo and Cross (1993) mention such an alternative that assesses skill in summarizing and also provides information on learning progress. At the end of a learning activity, each person writes a one sentence summary of what he or she learned. Learners may use as many clauses as they wish, but they are limited to one sentence. That limitation introduces a game-like quality that is desirable in assessing any aspect of the learning process.

Basic Academic Skills

Homework assignments can serve as a way to make assessments of learning progress for virtually every cell in the grid. They are especially appropriate for assessing basic academic skills. In a program to train workers to write effective business letters, an obvious homework assignment would be to write a business letter. The letters can be examined not only to see that they conform to the principles of this type of writing but also to assess the basic composition skills of the learners.

Discipline-Specific Knowledge and Skills

Homework assignments are equally effective in assessing progress in acquiring discipline-specific skills and knowledge. In order for them to work well, they need to be designed with the same care as formal learning activities. Similarly, they should be presented to the learners in considerable detail, preferably in writing. They should be fully integrated with other aspects of the learning program, and they should provide intellectual challenges not merely opportunities to memorize information or exercise basic academic skills. They can be personalized, but they must be critiqued by either an educator or by peers. In situations where grades will be assigned, homework assignments should probably count for some significant fraction of each learner's grade.

Pop quizzes also give reliable information on the progress of all the learners in a group, and they are not very time consuming. To avoid anxiety and morale problems, such quizzes probably should not be graded. One especially painless even playful way of conducting them is to use the All Thumbs format. The procedure is for the educator to read a list of true/false

questions. After each question, the learners give a thumbs up
sign if they think the statement is true and thumbs down if they
think it is false. They hold their thumbs close to their hearts so
others will not be influenced by seeing the signs. The educator
quickly counts the signs to check on learning progress and then
gives the correct sign for all to see.

Liberal Arts Values

Assessing progress toward acquiring liberal arts values can
be significantly different from assessing the learning of factual
material. One technique is to make anecdotal notes of the comments, conclusions, and divisions among learners during discussions of value-laden material. A comparison of notes from
points early and late in a learning program should reveal if progress toward a broader worldview has been made. Since learners
are not aware that the notes are being taken, such documentation can be particularly useful for assessing the actual senti-
ments of the learners. It is important that the notes be taken
systematically to get an accurate record of learners' expressed
opinions.

Work Preparation

Work preparation can be assessed with end of activity requests for the attitudes and opinions of the learners. For example, ask learners to hand in statements about what constitutes
good leadership or what is the difference between a good worker
and a poor worker. Their statements would indicate their comprehension of work-related issues as well as their opinions.

Personal Development

Assessing personal development is perhaps the most problematic of all informal assessments. Educators must be careful
not to intrude on the private lives of learners. On the other hand,

educators should not steadfastly veer away from the personal issues that matter so much to learners. Therefore, it seems appropriate for educators to invite answers to such rather broad questions as: What have you learned about yourself as a result of this learning program? Asking such questions requires educators to give thoughtful responses to learners and sometimes to reciprocate by answering the same question about themselves.

In general, the issue of assessing personal development is at least as much the province of the learners as of the educator. For that reason it is discussed more fully in Chapter 7 as part of the section on self-assessment.

ONE FINAL TECHNIQUE

A discussion of one last technique serves as a summary for assessing the learning process. The technique was described and named the "Muddiest Point" by Angelo and Cross (1993). It begins when a presenter asks a group of learners to write out what they experienced as the muddiest point in a presentation. The responses enable the presenter to determine whether learning difficulties existed and, if so, whether they were associated with an ineffective presentation (an assessment of learning activities), inattention on the part of the learners (an assessment of learning behaviors), inherently difficult material (a measure of learning progress), or all three.

The versatility of the technique is a reminder that a single technique can be used for more than one cell in the planning grid. It is also a reminder that a single assessment can serve many purposes allowing educators to plan only a small number of learning process assessments and still obtain several types of information from each.

The tone of the name highlights for the learners that assessment can have a playful side. It also suggests that no one is expected to be perfect and all people, the educator and themselves included, are wise to seek out and participate in assessing their own performance.

An educator who is told what was muddiest about a presentation should immediately try to clarify the point. The single most important factor in the success of any assessment of the learning process is the extent to which its results are used as feedback for improving learning. The results should be interpreted and shared with learners as soon as possible after they are obtained because their impact on the educator and on the learners declines over time. It may be that the results of a particular assessment are ambiguous. Sharing the ambiguity with the learners and planning follow-up activities are likely to be worthwhile.

WHAT IS NEXT

Chapter 2 focused on formative assessment for all six types of learning goals. The remaining chapters deal almost exclusively with summative assessment of thinking skills, basic academic skills, and discipline-specific learning goals. Although the terms and principles of formative and summative assessment are not terribly different, the procedures for summative assessments are more detailed because summative assessment is meant to be conclusive.

CHAPTER 3

Designing Relevant Tests

This chapter introduces the topic of testing with the following brief quiz:

Traditional paper and pencil tests are

1. continually criticized by professional educators

2. typically threatening to adult learners

3. often valid and reliable indicators of achievement

4. all of the above

Yes, the answer is 4, all of the above. And since all of the above are not only correct, but seemingly contradictory, some explaining is in order.

Traditional paper and pencil tests are composed of objective items and essay questions. They are often called meaningless because people are almost never asked to take such tests outside the classroom. They are sometimes called demeaning because they seem to assume that the learners might be able to repeat what has been imparted to them, but certainly cannot contribute worthwhile ideas of their own. On the other hand, these paper and pencil tests have been in use for centuries, and that longevity is an indication that they have a place in assessing adult learning. It seems a good guess that the dissatisfactions with classical paper and pencil tests are in large part the result of improper use. Therefore, this chapter focuses on determining when paper and pencil tests should be used and how they can be used properly.

APPROPRIATE USES OF
PAPER AND PENCIL TESTS

Assessment procedures should be chosen for use in a particular situation because they are compatible with what and how the learners have been learning. In general, paper and pencil tests would be the appropriate choice for evaluating learning that was conducted: (1) in a teacher-centered format; (2) with dependent learners; and/or (3) when the learning goal is to develop basic competence in a content area that is new to the learners. Examples of such goals include memorizing facts and procedures, understanding competing theories, solving technical problems, and analyzing arguments. Other techniques, which are covered in subsequent chapters, are generally more appropriate for assessing: self-directed learning, creative efforts, and complex performances. Examples are conducting a research project, writing a poem, repairing electronic equipment, and playing the violin.

PLANNING A TEST

The first step toward a successful test is integrating the planning of the test with the planning of the learning activities. The integration begins by stating the learning objectives that the learners are to pursue. A most useful way to conceive of learning objectives is from the standpoint of the Taxonomy of Educational Objectives (Bloom, Engelhart, Furst, Hill, & Krathwohl, 1956). The taxonomy is composed of three domains: cognitive, affective, and psychomotor. They are used analogously in planning both learning and assessment activities. In the interest of efficiency, only the cognitive domain is used in the illustrations that follow.

The cognitive domain was selected because it seems to have more direct applications for adult education than either of the others. It should be noted that the psychomotor domain is applicable whenever learners are concerned with physical skills such as those in volleyball or ballet. The affective domain is relevant in programs designed to produce attitude change such as alcohol education. However, the cognitive domain is almost always applicable in adult education because it deals with ways of knowing.

The Cognitive Domain

The cognitive domain is composed of six ways of knowing. They are listed below with the relatively more concrete presented first and the relatively more abstract last.

1. Knowledge is primarily a matter of memory for material previously learned.

2. Comprehension refers to acquiring an understanding of material without developing novel ideas of one's own.

3. Application means using knowledge and comprehension in order to solve problems.

4. Analysis refers to identifying the components of a unit and the interrelationships of the components. It is very close to what is meant by the phrase, critical thinking.

5. Synthesis involves gathering information and combining it into a whole. It is a creative process.

6. Evaluation refers to judging the relative quality of products and processes.

In general, the more abstract the level the more difficult the intellectual task. For example, it is easier to memorize the definition of a word (knowledge) than to use it correctly in a sentence (application). Similarly, it is likely to be easier to understand a sonnet (comprehension) than to write one (synthesis). This general rule often does not hold across different content areas. For example, most people would have a more difficult time solving calculus problems (application) than in criticizing the letters to the editors of their local newspaper (analysis). It is worth noting

	KNOW-LEDGE	COMPRE-HENSION	APPLI-CATION	ANALYSIS	SYN-THESIS	EVALUA-TION
TOPIC 1						
TOPIC 2						
TOPIC 3						

Figure 3.1 Test Planning Grid

that in Bloom's thinking, evaluation is the highest level. It implies that learning to evaluate one's own achievements is not only emotionally but intellectually difficult. It might be expected that learners would need extensive training in order to achieve competence in evaluating their work. It also seems that it would be an appropriately challenging task for virtually all learners.

The Test Planning Grid

In Chapter 2, a planning grid for scheduling formative assessments was described. At this point a grid for planning the content of summative assessments, including paper and pencil tests, is introduced. This grid is used to plan both learning and assessment activities. The levels in the cognitive domain form the top margin in the table, and the outline of the subject matter forms the left margin of the table. The planning process seems to work best if the content outline is a list of three to five roughly comparable topics. A sample grid is presented in Figure 3.1.

Using the Grid

The educator begins by using the grid as a checklist, considering each cell, beginning with the row for "Topic 1" and moving from the column headed "Knowledge" to the column headed "Evaluation." If the planner decides that the learners should memorize such things as definitions or dates associated with the "Topic 1," then in that first cell are entered the percentage of learning time that will be devoted to memorizing and the learning activities that seem best suited to accomplishing the memorization. The planner continues across the grid, making entries for other levels in the taxonomy, and then repeats the process for the remaining topics.

This process is clearly part of planning the learning activities, and it is also the beginning of the assessment planning because the percentage of learning time assigned to an objective is also the percentage of the test devoted to assessing that outcome. For example, if 30% of learning time is spent memorizing vocabulary in a foreign language course, then 30% of the test should assess knowledge of vocabulary. (In this context, learning time includes time spent in class meetings, independent studies, group projects and any other efforts directed toward reaching objectives.)

An actual planning grid is presented in Figure 3.2. Three parenting topics have been listed in the left margin. The educator has filled in the cells to identify the learning goals for the group. He or she has written in a brief description of the learning activity and the percentage of instructional time that will be devoted to each learning goal. The designation in the very first cell indicates that a lecture augmented with handouts will cover "Causes of Misbehavior" at the knowledge level and it will consume approximately 10% of learning time. Therefore, 10% of the test will cover "Causes of Misbehavior" at the knowledge level.

Several cells in the planning grid were bypassed. This is the usual situation rather than the exception. Cells might be bypassed because they do not encompass the goals of the learners or because they are subsumed under higher level objectives. In Figure 3.2, the planner does want the learners to understand the causes of misbehavior, but the comprehension would be covered adequately in the training for and assessment of analyzing vignettes which is designated in the fourth cell in row one.

	KNOW-LEDGE	COMPRE-HENSION	APPLI-CATION	ANALYSIS	SYN-THESIS	EVALUA-TION
CAUSES OF MISBEHAV-IOR	lecture & handout 10%			discuss vignette 10%		
PRINCIPLES OF DISCIPLINE		demon-stration & handout 20%	small group problem solving 20%			
EFFECTIVE COMMUNI-CATION	lecture & handout 10%		role-play 10%			discuss role-play 20%

Figure 3.2 Test Planning Grid for Parenting Education

Although knowledge-level objectives are rarely the outcomes of greatest interest, they are almost always the focus of some learning and assessment activities because simple knowledge outcomes form the basis for higher-level thinking. Therefore, one of the important tasks for the planner is to construct and then revise the grid until the proper blend of knowledge and higher level objectives has been achieved. There is no formula for determining the proper blend. Nonetheless, educators seem to achieve a relatively more appropriate blend of knowledge and higher level objectives for a given learning situation when they use a planning grid than when they do not.

Without the grid there is a tendency for learning and assessment activities to become anchored to lower-level objectives perhaps because it is easier to write test items at the knowledge level than at higher levels. Using the planning grid virtually ensures that the test will be valid because there is correspondence between what was taught and studied and what will be tested. The correspondence is not only for content but level of cognition as well. The grid dictates that when learners study at the analysis level they are assessed at the analysis level.

Using a grid also goes a long way toward creating an adequate test. The term adequate is used here in the technical sense. It does not mean that the test is "good enough." It means that all the important learning objectives are covered in enough detail that test results are a good indication of how well an individual learner has achieved those objectives. After all, if an important objective were to learn a set of 25 definitions, but only 3 definitions were tested, the results would be meaningless because it is possible that the 3 definitions tested were the only definitions the person knew or did not know. The term adequate is also a reminder that overkill is not a virtue. If all objectives were tested to the furthest extent possible, assessment would become so time-consuming that it would crowd out learning activities. The grid is an aid in asking the right number of questions about the important learning objectives.

The Test Outline

Once the grid has been finished, both the learning and the assessment activities must be planned in detail. Given the focus of this book on assessment, no additional space can be allotted for planning learning activities. Assuming that stellar activities have been planned, the next step in planning the test is to construct the test outline. The purpose of the test outline is to specify what the learners will be doing when they are answering test questions. It indicates whether the learners will be matching items, filling in blanks, writing essays, and so forth. The sample in Figure 3.3 illustrates the features of a test outline.

The first level in the outline, marked by the Roman numerals, is composed of the content topics from the left margin in the planning grid. The second level—the capital letters—is composed of the levels in the taxonomy from the top margin of the grid. The third level—the Arabic numbers—is what is new. It consists of descriptions of what the learners will be doing when they demonstrate their achievement of the objectives.

In Figure 3.3, at the Knowledge level for Causes of Misbe-

  I. Causes of Misbehavior
     A. Knowledge
        1. Matches terms to definitions
        2. Recognizes correct statements regarding causes of
           misbehavior
     B. Analysis
        1. Selects correct causes of misbehavior in scenarios
 II. Principles of Discipline
     A. Comprehension
        1. Explains principles in own words
     B. Application
        1. Recommends disciplinary action for specified offenses
III. Effective Communication
     A. Knowledge
        1. Defines terms
        2. Matches terms to definitions
     B. Application
        1. Recommends responses to child's statements
     C. Evaluation
        1. Assesses statements by parents to children in scenarios

Figure 3.3 Test Outline for Parenting Education

havior are two descriptions of learner behavior. The first, "Matches terms to definitions," actually includes no reference to any content. It could be used for virtually any knowledge level objective, and it does appear twice in the sample outline in the figure. This type of description of learner behavior is often recommended because it makes writing a three-level outline a short job, with additional savings in time and effort when it is used on subsequent outlines. The second description, "recognizes correct statements of facts pertaining to causes of misbehavior," contains specific mention of content. Whereas this type of description can rarely be used for more than one objective, it makes writing test questions a simple matter of rewriting the description of learner behavior. There is no reason to use only one type of description although it appears that experienced test writers prefer the reusable variety that omits mention of subject matter content.

WRITING TEST ITEMS

Educators can normally write the test items directly from the outline because the descriptions of learner behaviors in the third level of the outline designate the important learning outcomes for the group, and they imply the form of the test items. For example, in Figure 3.3 under Causes of Misbehavior at the Knowledge level, the learner behavior is "matches terms to definitions" so an educator would write a set of matching items with terms in one column and definitions in the other. Further down where the outline calls for learners to explain, an educator would develop an essay question. When it calls for learners to recognize, an educator would write multiple-choice items.

In addition to working directly from the outline, educators should follow well-established guidelines for writing individual items. The following guidelines pertain to virtually all types of test items:

- Write all items in the simplest, most direct language.
- Avoid ambiguities.
- Avoid clues to correct answers.
- Solicit a review of the test from a colleague.
- Continually upgrade a file of test items.

These guidelines are not entirely self-explanatory, so they are elaborated below.

Using Simple Direct Language

Professional educators naturally write test items with standard spelling, punctuation, and grammar, but they sometimes fail to keep items easy to understand. They are well advised to write every item with the fewest and the simplest words that convey their meaning in order to minimize reading and language skills as a barrier to successful performance on the test. If learners are being challenged by the learning objectives, they should be given aid and comfort by every other aspect of the assessment process, including the number and complexity of the words in the test items. For example, "Should the committee buy the property?" is preferable to "Should the committee move ahead with the decision to conclude the purchase of the property in question?"

Avoiding Ambiguities

On occasion, the guidelines for writing items may seem to conflict as is the case when using the fewest words might lead to ambiguities. In such cases, avoiding the ambiguities would take precedence. For example, "Who discovered America?" appears to be a simple direct question, well posed in the fewest possible words, but a better question would be "Who is generally considered the first to sail from Europe to America and back?" This is not a matter of being politically correct, it is a matter of being certain that all learners understand the item the same way. It eliminates the confusion caused when learners answer Leif Eriksson, St. Brendan, nobody really knows, or people crossing a land bridge from Asia to Alaska when the educator is convinced the answer is Christopher Columbus.

Avoiding Clues

Avoiding clues is a pressing concern on tests with objective items. The underlying concern is to have tests that measure achievement of learning objectives without measuring a learner's ability to take tests. Clues come in a variety of forms. Sometimes they are within an item; for example, the grammar of a multiple-choice item might allow the test takers to eliminate one or more of the options for the answer. True/false items are likely to contain clues in the qualifiers that are attached to the main statement. Qualifiers like "in general" or "with some exceptions" hint that statements are true while "always" and "never" hint they are false.

On other occasions there are clues between items. An example, hopefully not too obvious, would be found if one question were "Who is generally considered the first to sail from Europe to America and back?" and a subsequent question were "From what continent did Columbus sail when he discovered America?"

Soliciting Reviews from Colleagues and Stakeholders

After an educator has taken all steps to produce a good test, it is good practice to have a colleague critique the test. Although a critique is not needed for a 10-minute quiz that would be used in formative assessment of the learning process, it is appropriate whenever a major test is given, a substantial number of new test items were written, or there have been problems with previous tests.

It may also be beneficial to solicit critiques from people outside the learning setting. For example, if learners are in a job training program, it might be wise to ask potential employers or supervisors to examine the test, its planning grid, and three-level outline to ensure that the most significant learning outcomes are being addressed in assessment as well as in learning activities.

Upgrading the Test File

Writing good tests is difficult so educators should recycle their test items. This does not mean reusing a test time and time again. It means developing a large pool of items for each learning objective by writing new items, saving successful items, improving items that have caused problems, and writing altered forms for existing items. For example, take a good true/false item where the answer is false and write a comparable item on the same material where the answer is true, and store both. When it is time to construct a test, draw items from the test pool that will be significantly different from and hopefully better than those used last time. Recycling test items is a simple method for improving tests.

GUIDELINES FOR TYPES OF TEST ITEMS

Another set of guidelines consists of suggestions for writing different types of test items. To this point, the terms objective items and essay questions have been used to differentiate among types of testing approaches. These terms were used because they are in common usage. But here at the beginning of a review of the different types of items, it becomes helpful to replace them with the terms select items and supply items respectively.

Writing Select Type Items

Select items require a learner to select a correct answer from among two or more choices that are presented as part of the items. Below is a list of the types of select items along with guidelines for writing each type.

Matching Items

Matching items are usually most helpful for measuring simple knowledge-level objectives. They are relatively easy to write: premises are put in column A with the responses in column B. Learners are asked to write the premise from column A next to its matching response in column B. There is usually no problem putting matching exercises in simple language, but problems do arise when learners are asked to match large numbers of items because the task becomes a measure of ability to juggle information in one's head as much as a measure of what knowledge one has gained. It is always best to know from experience how many matches would be too many for a particular group. In the absence of such experience, it is a good idea to limit the number of matches to five or six.

The most common problem with matching items is the subtle cluing that occurs when the items to be matched come from very different content areas. Consider the following exercise where learners are to match leaders of the 1990s in column A to their leadership roles in column B:

Column A	Column B
Pope John Paul	Russian leader
Hillary Clinton	religious leader
Boris Yeltsin	U.S. health care reformer

It is possible to answer correctly without ever having heard of any of these leaders. A pope is a good bet to be a religious leader. The most Russian sounding name should be the Russian leader, and the remaining items can be linked by the process of elimination. Of course, this is a caricature of a matching exercise; however, it illustrates some of the clues that creep into matching exercises. By confining matching exercises to a single content area such as authors and the books they wrote with at least one response in column B that does not match any of the premises in column A, the problem of unintended clues can be controlled.

At first glance, the concern with people getting the correct answer without having learned the material might reinforce the notion that educators who do testing are simply against giving anybody a break. Actually, the concern is with remaining true to the purpose of assessing learning accurately so that when learners achieve well, there is cause to celebrate and when they do not, there is reason to alter their learning activities and/or learning behaviors. There is no sense in allowing clues in test items to overestimate learning achievement and thereby overlooking ways to improve learning.

True/False Items

True/false items are actually a special case of alternative-response items. Alternative-response items are those questions where learners are asked to express a judgment using two (occasionally more than two) options. In addition to indicating whether a statement is true or false, alternative-response items are used to ask whether a statement is a matter of fact or opinion, whether a conclusion is supported by the information given or not supported by the information given, and so on. Surprisingly, alternative-response items are sometimes maligned for being mindless measures of memory when actually they can be very useful for assessing higher-level thinking.

Alternative-response items seem relatively easy to write. One pitfall resides in the fact that very few important statements are always true or always false, unequivocally valid or invalid, and so forth. Consider the following true/false item that might be used for the learning goal I-A-2 in Figure 3.3, "Recognizes correct statements regarding causes of misbehavior": "Boys have more developmental problems than girls." Some people would say true because on average boys have more developmental problems than girls. Others would think that boys usually have more developmental problems but not every boy has more problems than every girl so they refrain from answering true. One solution is to use a qualifier. "In general, boys have more developmental problems than girls."

This solution is more apparent than real. The term "in general" belongs with other phrases like "for the most part" and "on the whole" which are fairly reliable clues that the item is true. Such clues are undesirable. Similarly, the item "Boys always have more developmental problems than girls" is a bad item because the term "always" is a clue that the answer is false. Neither is it acceptable to write, "In general, girls have more developmental problems than boys" because the test writer is using the qualifier to deceive the test takers.

There is a satisfactory solution: change from a traditional true/false item to a simple question. "In general, do boys or girls have more developmental problems?" The choices for answers will, of course, change to "(1) Boys, (2) Girls, and (3) Neither." With the exception of matching items, the simple question is often the most effective way of presenting a test item.

Occasionally, alternative-response items contain two propositions for the learner to judge. "Boys generally have more developmental problems than girls, but are they more obedient than girls." This item cannot be answered with a single response. It illustrates the importance of having only one proposition in an alternative-response item.

True/false items can become excruciating if they include complicated sentences or if they include negatives. For example: "Never include negatives in a true/false item, unless it is necessary to do so in order to measure achievement of an important learning objective." The answer is unequivocally true. But confronting 25 such items would be frustrating, possibly to the point of depressing a person's performance. It is far better to use: "Minimize the use of negatives in true/false items."

Multiple-Choice Items

Multiple-choice items are extremely versatile. They can be used to measure knowledge, comprehension, application, and analysis at least as easily as other types of items. They are also among the most difficult to write. They consist of a stem and options (usually four), of which one must be chosen as the correct answer. At the very least, there is a lot to write, and for the person taking the test, a lot to read. It is therefore, important to try to simplify the items. One method for simplifying is to put as much information as possible in the stem and as little as possible in the options.

Avoiding clues to correct answers is extremely important. Generally, any factor that draws attention to an item can serve as a clue. For example, if the correct answer is longer or shorter than the other options, if it contains the sort of qualifiers often found in true/false items, if it sounds more like a textbook, if its grammar matches the stem, then testwise adults will be able to pick out the correct answer without having achieved the learning objective.

One of the most commonly occurring clues to the correct answer on multiple-choice tests is also one of the easiest to correct. It has to do with the location of the correct answer among the options. Individual test writers seem to develop a habit of placing the correct answer as either second or third among the four options. Testwise adults will take advantage of that habit. It is a simple matter to review a test after it is written and scramble the location of the correct answers.

Multiple-choice items sometimes contain more than one option that could be considered a correct answer although one would be considered the best answer. These are called "best answer type" as opposed to the "correct answer type" which have only one answer that could be seen as right. The best answer type is sometimes recommended for assessing higher mental processes, but can be demoralizing to learners. It seems wise to avoid them or use them only when there is a compelling reason to do so.

Multiple-choice items have one distinct advantage over other select items. They offer the opportunity to analyze the incorrect answers in order to detect the learners' misconceptions, and subsequently correct them. For example:

1. Pig : Peccary : : Dog :
   a. chicken   b. cat   c. dolphin   d. wolf

A learner who gives an incorrect answer immediately causes an educator to hypothesize about the problem. If someone answered a chicken, he or she might not know what a peccary is or might not know what an analogy is. The answer cat, suggests the person may use associations instead of logic. The hypotheses could be tested against other incorrect answers, and presumably lead to an understanding of the learner's strengths and weaknesses.

Interpretive Exercises

An interpretive exercise is a set of select items specifically designed to measure achievement at the higher levels in Bloom's taxonomy. Each exercise is composed of a an array of information that is new to the people taking the test and a set of items about that array of information. The array of information can take almost any form. It could be written text, a poem, a photograph, a graph, a map, or whatever form information takes in the field being studied. The items may be alternative-response or multiple-choice. Since the information in the array is new to the test takers, they are not asked knowledge-level items, but they are asked to process the information using the thinking skills they are trying to develop in their learning activities.

For example, here is an interpretive exercise that might be used to assess the learning goal in Figure 3.3, I-B-1—"Selects correct causes of misbehavior from among alternatives":

Read the following description and answer questions 1 and 2 based on your analysis of the description.

> John has gone to the grocery store with his parents and younger brother, Tim. His mother says that John will get a reward if he can behave as well as Tim does. As they go up and down the aisles, his mother says Tim is the quietest boy in the store. Several times his father reminds John to talk softly and leave things on the shelves. As they pass the display of breakfast foods, John picks up a large box of cereal, runs down the aisle, and crashes into Tim who has his back to John.

> 1. Which one of the remarks from his parents seems most likely to have contributed to John's misbehavior?
>   A. His mother saying he would get a reward if he behaved as well as Tim.
> * B. His mother saying Tim is the quietest boy in the store.
>   C. His father reminding him to talk softly.
>   D. His father reminding him to leave things on the shelves.
> 2. Which seems to have been John's motive for misbehaving?
>   A. Revenge
>   B. Greed
>   C. Control
> * D. Attention

This example contains only two questions in order to save space. Normally, interpretive exercises contain five or more questions. Nonetheless, it illustrates the principle of presenting novel information and asking test takers to process that information. It also demonstrates that interpretive exercises are somewhat difficult to write. The items must meet the usual demands for simplicity and clarity without clues to the correct answers.

Therefore, an educator who develops an interpretive exercise should enter it into a test item pool so that it can be used repeatedly. It may be refined and expanded, but it should be recycled so that the amount of time and energy spent developing the exercise will not be repeated.

In order to reuse test items, an educator must have reason to believe that the items have not been surreptitiously shared by any of the people taking the test. The concern is typically nonexistent unless grades or some similar evaluation of learner performance are based on the test results. An educator who bases evaluations even in part on the basis of test results and wants to reuse test items should have a system for maintaining test security. One of the simplest is to hand test sheets directly to individuals who are taking the test. As long as the test takers record their names and at least some test answers on the test sheet— essays, or fill-in-the-blank type items—the educator will be able to collect all of the test sheets, thereby maintaining test security for test administration.

The one drawback to this system comes in providing learners with quick feedback for their performance on a test. Since returning tests would jeopardize security, test takers should record their answers on a separate sheet which can be returned to them while they view a single copy of the exam (perhaps projected on a screen) and correct answers are explained.

Supply Items

Supply items are items for which the test takers produce the response from their own resources. Among supply items there are two varieties which are discussed separately: short answer and essay questions.

Short Answer Items

The short answer items take one of two forms. The first is the direct question: "Who is generally considered the first to sail from Europe to America and back?" The second is the fill-in-the-blank or completion item: "The person who is usually considered to be the first to sail from Europe to America and back was _____." These items are relatively easy to write, and the direct question is, as the comparison indicates, often the easier one for test takers to understand. They have much in common with multiple-choice items while relieving the test maker of writing the options. Perhaps the major problem with these short answer items is that they are surprisingly difficult to score objectively if there is the least bit of ambiguity in the test item itself.

As a result, multiple-choice items are generally a better choice than short answer items. However, short answer items are recommended in two situations. The first is whenever calculations are required and giving options would be likely to serve as clues to the correct answers. The second is when recall of information is clearly important. For example, we might think that emergency medical technicians should be able to recall what to do in the case of a heart attack, not merely select what to do if they are asked which option to pick.

Essay Questions

Essay questions are among the most effective means of assessing the higher levels of the cognitive domain. They may be the item of choice for assessing a person's ability to select and organize information. In planning to fully exploit the power of essay questions, it is helpful to distinguish between structured and unstructured essays. "Compare teacher-centered and learner-centered education" is a relatively unstructured essay topic. If it were followed by: "Be sure to address the following questions: Who designs the learning activities? What is the role of assessment? In which settings are they likely to be more effective?" then it would be a structured essay.

The structured essay seems to have the advantage of including all the information that a learner needs in order to respond. In fact, experienced educators know that the structured format leads to essays that are easier to rank from best to worst, are more likely to address the main issues covered in the learning activities, are of higher quality overall, and are less likely to have learners saying, "I didn't know what you wanted." For some educators the experience is so much more positive with the structured format that they refer to structured essays as improved essays.

On the other hand, the structured essay has a major disadvantage. As an essay question becomes more structured, it is the question maker and not the essayist who is selecting and organizing the information. The essay question is measuring recall not the important learning objectives of selecting and organizing information, and the apparently good performance of the learners on the structured essay may be misleading. From this perspective, it appears that the unstructured essay is more effective for the important job of assessing higher mental processes such as synthesis.

There may be a resolution to the apparent dilemma over the choice of structured or unstructured essays questions. The structured essay can be used as an educational tool. It may be recommended for use with more dependent, less sophisticated learners to assess expression of what they recall, and to train them in the skills of selecting and organizing information. With more self-directed, sophisticated learners, the unstructured essay would seem more appropriate.

Scoring essays is challenging and essay questions should not be administered unless the educator has a clear idea of how they will be scored. In fact, scoring considerations might necessitate changes in what looks like a sound question at first glance. The procedures for scoring essays are discussed in Chapter 4. Here we turn to the remaining factor in test design, which is preparing learners to take tests.

PREPARING LEARNERS TO TAKE TESTS

Taking tests is an important skill that some people acquire on their own, and other people can acquire from direct instruction. It seems wise for educators to work toward achieving some kind of equality in the test-taking skills of the learners they plan to assess. Otherwise, what look like differences in achievement among learners may simply be differences in test taking skills. Some guidelines for helping learners improve their test taking follow.

Objective Tests

The test-taking skills that apply to objective items are: survey the test to allot time for all questions. When tests include objective and essay questions, answer the objective questions first. Identify clues to the right answers, and answer all questions even if it means guessing. On multiple-choice questions, eliminate as many options as possible and guess among the remaining options.

Essay Tests

Since learners are likely to have different skills in writing essay answers, it makes sense to provide learning activities that help all the members of a group become proficient in writing them. Furthermore, even people who have taken professional licensing examinations report that specific training in writing essay exams would have helped them. Specific directions include read the question carefully and pay particular attention to those verbs such as compare, list, describe, and justify. Write an outline of the answer including definitions for terms. Revise the outline, making sure it is legible. Write the answer from the outline then edit it. If time runs out, hand in the legible outline along with the unfinished essay.

In addition to the specific directions, educators should consider giving learners opportunities to analyze strong and weak answers to essay questions.

Preparing for a Particular Test

There is a long tradition in educational psychology of arguing that learners should have a clear idea of what is going to be on a test. There has not been consensus on how to convey that information to learners. For adult learners, it seems that educators could first share the planning grid and then the three-level outline of the test. This is not commonly done, and at first it would be time-consuming to explain the levels in the taxonomy, but it would seem to have many benefits. Not only would it put learners in a position to prepare for the test adequately and efficiently, but it would model for them the logic of their assessment activities. Adult learners who are given the power of knowing how tests are developed could provide input into planning their tests. This would be a healthy development because the experience would train them to identify and pursue important learning objectives as well as monitor their own progress as they complete their self-directed learning contracts.

As a final means of preparing adults to take a test, educators would do well to give out sample items from the test. This step is especially important if the test contains item types that may be unfamiliar such as interpretive exercises and other higher-level questions. The sample items and all other materials intended to prepare learners to take a test should be distributed as far ahead of the test date as possible because people will adapt their study habits to what they believe will be expected of them. If they expect to be tested only on definitions, they will limit their study to committing definitions to memory. If they see examples of interpretive exercises, they will spend time practicing higher level thinking skills. Both their performance and their morale will be improved.

Taking the Anxiety out of Testing

Many adults are anxious about being assessed and that anxiety can impair performance. Whereas some test anxiety may be helpful, it can easily rise to where it leaves some adults seriously disadvantaged. Relieving people of time pressure by scheduling ample testing time is one of the easiest ways to reduce anxiety. There are few paper and pencil tests for which people should be under time pressure. In cases where it seems important to limit the scope of the responses as it might on an essay test, it would be preferable to limit the number of pages test takers may write rather than the amount of time they have. Except in situations where it is important to assess simple memory for information, anxiety can be reduced by conducting open-book and open-notes tests.

There are test administration practices that also reduce anxiety. First is to give the test in a low-key, friendly, but business-like fashion. Second, provide clear written directions for each section of the test. Third, minimize distractions. The fourth is sometimes called the Academic Anxiety Reduction Procedure (AARP). The AARP is an attempt to reduce the problem, common to adult learners, of reading too much into a test question. It works in the following manner: when test takers believe they know the material being tested but find the test item confusing, they select an answer and then write on their test question sheet a short explanation of what they know and why they believe the question is confusing. They are then graded on their explanations. Rarely does anyone write out such an explanation more than three times on a test, and most people write none at all. Nonetheless, the opportunity creates a clear sense that the test is measuring what they know and not how easily they can be tricked.

Every effort should be made to lower the stakes associated with the outcomes of testing. The stakes might be a grade in a course or support for an application for a promotion. In such cases, one way to lower the stakes is to have multiple tests and grades based on nontest assessments so that no single test is a make or break situation. Not only does this practice relieve anxiety, but it is good assessment practice because educational tests are not precise enough to justify making an important decision about a person based on just one test. The stakes can also be personal in the sense that adult learners may base their self-esteem on their performances. Therefore, discussions of tests should minimize comparisons among individuals in favor of highlighting the progress of the learners and the use of the tests as feedback for improving learning.

The most general principle is that healthy individuals do not want risk-free situations. They want to be faced with intellectually challenging tasks as long as they perceive that they have a fair chance to succeed. Therefore, well-designed and well-administered tests are not a threat but a boost to the self-esteem and morale of learners.

Some Questionable Practices

Some cautions for those trying to take the anxiety out of testing follow: take-home exams reduce anxiety because they are open-book tests with no time limits, but they should be avoided whenever there is a possibility they might tempt learners to get help from others. Allowing test takers to choose among essays is thought to reduce worry of being struck dumb by a single unexpected question. However, there is a risk that allowing choices among essays will encourage learners to gamble that they will know enough about some of the questions to get a satisfactory score without studying all the material. So, when choices among essays are given, plan for some other means of ensuring that all test takers address all the material covered in the learning activities. An extensive set of objective questions may do very well.

LOOKING AHEAD

After a sound test has been designed and administered in a professional matter, there are several tasks for the educator to address. The results must be used to assess the learners, the learning activities, and even the test itself. These topics are addressed in Chapter 4. In subsequent chapters, consideration is given to what additional or alternative methods of assessment are suitable for the learning goals of the learners.

CHAPTER 4

Making the Most of Test Results

The systematic test planning procedures that were described in Chapter 3 must be matched with equally precise methods for scoring.

SCORING TESTS

Ideally, scoring should be objective in the sense that a given test would receive the same score regardless of who does the scoring. Whereas objectivity is a constant goal, it is more attainable for select than for supply test items.

Scoring Select Items

Matching, alternative-response, and multiple-choice items are relatively simple to score because each item was written to have one and only one correct answer. Scoring usually consists of assigning one point for each correct answer. One variation is to weight answers so that a learner might receive one point for correct responses to some items, but receive two, three, or more points for correct answers to other items. Educators sometimes weight items when they believe that the items measure learning outcomes of different importance. There may be some situations where weighting is appropriate. However, if a test has been planned with a grid, the more important learning outcomes will be assessed with proportionately more items, and weighting would be an unnecessary complication.

A second variation is to correct each person's score by estimating how many items a person got right simply by guessing and then subtracting that number from the person's total of correct answers. On a test of true/false items, a person would get one right for every one wrong—50% correct on the test. The correction for guessing is made by subtracting one point for each incorrect answer so that a person who merely guessed would receive a zero. In the eyes of some, the zero is appropriate because the person could not do better than someone who learned nothing and flipped coins to select answers. By the same logic, if the items were four choice multiple-choice items, guessing would yield one correct response, and three incorrect responses for every four items. The person who guessed on all the items would have 25% correct, but the person's total number correct would be reduced by 1/3 of the total of incorrect responses, and the person would receive a zero.

Correcting for guessing has some merit when it is done on published tests, but it has little merit when it is applied to tests made by individual educators. First, it is confusing for many adults, and may cause them to skip too many items simply because they are less than 100% confident of the answers. Second, correcting for guessing is time-consuming, especially when the test combines true/false, and multiple-choice items. Third, it lowers morale among the learners by suggesting that the educator is preoccupied with giving people the lowest possible score instead of giving them credit for what they have learned.

Scoring Supply Items

Scoring supply items objectively is difficult because there are no single objectively correct answers for any of them. Even scoring fill-in-the-blank items requires judgment. If the item were: America was discovered in 1492 by _____. Would any or all of the following be correct: Christopher Columbo, Christopher C., Christopher, Columbus, Columbia? Adding stipulations such as all answers must be spelled correctly and all names must include first and last names, may improve objectivity in scoring but often cause other problems. In this case, marking an answer incorrect based on a spelling error might be the wrong action when the test taker is trying his or her best to learn English as well as master the historical content. As indicated by this example, the difficulty of scoring completion items can be so great that many educators avoid them entirely.

Scoring Essays

Scoring essays is usually done according to either the point or the rating method. These methods share three important features. First, scorers should be unaware of who wrote an essay as they score it. Second, on tests with more than one essay question, score the answers to a single question at a time. Third, there should be more than one reader. Although this third condition is often difficult to fulfill, it goes a long way toward producing objective scores and in so doing it reassures test takers that their scores are accurate. Given its benefits, it is worth trying to establish partnerships in which educators read the essays written by one another's learners.

For the point system, the educator writes not only the essay question, but a model answer to the question. Each test taker's answer is compared to the model answer, and a specified number of points is assigned for each element in the test taker's essay that also appears in the model essay. This system is more successful with the structured type of essay because the structure directs all writers to address the same points.

In the rating system, the educator reads the essays and sorts them into groups based upon the reader's overall estimate of quality. This system can be used with almost any type of essay, but it is clearly the appropriate choice for scoring unstructured essays. Several guidelines for conducting this type of assessment follow:

- Score all essays under comparable conditions. The reader should be refreshed and free of preoccupations.
- Establish a single standard for assessing all essays by reading 25 percent or more of them to get an idea of how the group has done.
- Maintain the standard by scoring all the answers to any one question in one sitting.
- Sort essays into a small number of groups—four or five.

The purpose for scoring objective items is clear. It quickly informs people about what they have or have not accomplished. The same can be said about the point system for scoring essays. However, it is not the case with the rating system which simply provides an indication of the quality of an essay in relation to the other learners in the group. The rating system must be supplemented with careful critiques of individual essays if learners are to receive meaningful feedback about their progress. Of course, the ratings can be used for grading purposes, and those are discussed shortly.

Peripheral and Irrelevant Factors

Scores on essays are intended to reflect the extent to which individual learners have achieved the learning goals that were specified in the planning grid for summative assessment. One of the major threats to the validity of the scores is the impact of peripheral factors such as spelling, punctuation, handwriting, and bluffing on the scoring process.

Spelling and other mechanics of writing are particularly problematic. On the one hand, the score on the essay is supposed to reflect the achievement of learning goals, but on the other hand, effective composition is an overarching goal of all educational activities and should not be treated as irrelevant. One solution is to give separate scores for achieving the learning goals and for composition. This is most appropriate when good composition is a legitimate learning objective as it might be if learners were studying a foreign language and writing an essay in that language. When composition is not among the stated learning goals, it may be preferable to require test takers to correct writing errors in order to get a score for the learning objectives.

Irrelevant factors are often thought of as working to depress a person's score. However, they can work to inflate scores. Impeccable handwriting and well-crafted sentences can create a positive halo effect. In addition, there are strategies that can substitute for substance and raise scores. Among these are extolling the importance of the topic in the question, including truisms such as "further research is needed" and inserting compliments to the educator like "we have certainly learned a great deal about this topic in the last 2 months."

A good overall strategy for minimizing the impact of irrelevant factors on scoring is to paraphrase each essay. It would be desirable to write the paraphrase as an appendix to the essay, and include the main point(s), supporting evidence, and evidence that was omitted. This practice keeps the focus on the thinking process, provides feedback to the test taker, and promotes valid scoring. Mentioning it raises the larger question of giving feedback to learners on their essays.

Comments to Learners

One of the disappointments of essay exams is that they often result in assessments of how well a learner can select and organize information, but they do not promote progress in either selecting or organizing information because learners get brief comments and because they zero in on the grade. It is easy for educators and learners to become so concerned with valid assessment that the learning aspect is overlooked. Ideally, each essay should be returned with feedback that promotes skills in selecting and organizing information. No doubt, it is time-consuming, but it is important enough to warrant the time. The feedback should be a model of scholarly analysis.

In order to explore ways of providing feedback, a sample

essay question is presented, followed by some possible comments from a scorer. The essay question is Read the description of the financial situation of the Browns, then examine the following investment plan which has been developed for them. Describe the most important aspects of the plan and offer an overall evaluation of the plan.

Feedback on any individual essay should begin by describing in detail what was well done. For example, "Your organization was apparent and well done. Very wisely, you started by defining the terms. Then you stated that there were three important aspects of the issue, gave them each a number and devoted a separate paragraph to each. All three were well chosen and well analyzed."

The feedback should then address what was not so well done. For example, "There was a fourth point that you might have mentioned. It was. . . . I couldn't find the overall evaluation of the plan that was asked for in the question. What you wrote was good. I am wondering if you ran out of time and did not put the evaluation in for that reason."

The feedback should not be entirely scholarly or disinterested. It is addressed to a person who has a relationship with the scorer and who, at different times, is likely to have feelings from joy to shame about his or her learning. Therefore, the feedback should end with encouragement. Encouragement can take many forms. It might be a suggestion, such as "If you did run out of time, you could make a special effort to budget your time in more detail for the next test. On your next essay you might check for words like evaluate, contrast, outline, and describe, and build them into the beginning of your essay as a reminder of what the question is asking you to do. For example, if you had begun by saying, 'After describing the aspects of the program, I will offer an overall evaluation of the program,' you would guide yourself to answer exactly the question that was asked." Encouragement could also be pointing out progress. For example, "Generally, I think you are doing a better and better job of organizing material. Keep it up." Throughout the feedback, the educator should keep in mind that encouragement is more important than evaluation.

MAKING INTERPRETATIONS ABOUT INDIVIDUAL LEARNERS

Having discussed scoring and commenting on test performances, it is time to consider the formal means for interpreting an individual learner's test scores. The systems for doing so go by the rather lengthy names of criterion-referenced and norm-referenced interpretations. These terms were introduced in Chapter 1, and they are developed further at this point. (Self-referenced interpretations, also mentioned in Chapter 1, are not part of this discussion because it focuses on interpretations made by educators.)

Criterion-Referenced Interpretations

Criterion-referenced interpretations involve comparing a learner to some standard of accomplishment. Many adults find themselves evaluated in this fashion on a regular basis. Depending on their state of residence, licensed automobile drivers undergo a test to determine whether or not they are suitable to continue as licensed drivers. The testing might include a vision exam, a multiple-choice test on the laws regulating motor vehicles, and even a road test of physical skills such as driving around a city neighborhood under close observation of an inspector. In this evaluation, there is no need to determine exactly how much skill any individual has on any one measure. In particular, there is no need to determine how well one person does compared to another or to the group of licensed drivers as a whole. Whether a person knows the rules of the road better than 90% or 50% or 10% of the drivers is not important. All of the components of the assessment are interpreted on the basis of a criterion or standard or cutoff score. From the vision exam to the road test, the concern is whether or not the person performed well enough to avoid accidents.

The most complex aspect of criterion-referenced test interpretations is in setting the standard for acceptable accomplishment. Ideally, it should be an empirical matter. In the case of knowing the rules of the road, a research team would record scores on the test for a large group of people. The people would be followed in order to gather information regarding their driving records for some period of time, say 3 to 5 years. (In the extreme case, no one in the group would have been denied a license on the basis of the test score.) At the end of the period test scores and driving records would be compared. If higher scores on the test are associated with fewer violations and accidents, then a search for a cutoff score would be initiated. Ideally, the researchers would be able to identify a score that divides people into one group that has almost no accidents or violations and another group that has an unacceptable number of violations and accidents. That score would be called the cutoff or the standard or the criterion.

There are other situations in which it makes sense to rely on experts to determine what criteria should be used. For example, those with experience actually rescuing people from drowning are probably the best judges of what a potential lifeguard should know and be able to do before he or she is certified as a competent lifeguard.

In many educational situations, research and expert opinion on cutoff scores are lacking. In such cases, the usual practice is to adopt a score of approximately 85% as the criterion representing mastery. Often educational tests are made up of sections of distinct material which are called domains. On such tests, it is sometimes useful to assess learners for competence on the individual domains. If there are at least 10 questions within a domain, a score of approximately 85% correct on the items within that domain is probably an acceptable indicator of mastery of the domain.

Providing Feedback on Criterion-Referenced Tests

When learners are given feedback about their performance on criterion-referenced tests, they should be told whether or not they passed and they should be given:

- Their own score
- What the criterion is and how it was set
- Descriptions of any domains
- The domains they mastered and failed to master
- The items they answered correctly and incorrectly
- Encouragement and, if needed, recommendations for achieving mastery wherever they had not demonstrated it

Norm-Referenced Interpretations

Norm-referenced interpretations are made by comparing an individual's performance to the performance of others on the same test. "She scored higher than 90% of the applicants." "He performed as well as the average 12th grade student." These are both examples of norm-referenced interpretations. This is the system that is used for most published tests of academic achievement such as the Wide Range Achievement Test which measures spelling, arithmetic, and reading from first grade level on up, and the Graduate Record Examination which is used in assessing college graduates applying to graduate school.

Individual educators also make norm-referenced interpretations based on scores derived from their own tests. In fact, norm-referenced interpretations are appropriate whenever educators assess learners in content areas for which there are no unambiguous or objective criteria to indicate mastery. If a learner is preparing to be an Emergency Medical Technician, we expect that there are clear standards of mastery. But when a learner is preparing to be a counselor, we understand that there will not be unambiguous standards. In such cases it makes sense to assess individual learners in terms of the performance of other learners, and a learner who answers more questions correctly is perceived to be the more masterful.

One of the most complex issues in communicating to learners about their level of success on norm-referenced tests comes under the heading of item difficulty. This is not a particular problem in the area of criterion-referenced testing because the nature of the content being covered determines the item difficulty. For example, a test of procedures for cleaning a photo-copying machine probably would have fewer and easier items than a test for competence in repairing a photocopying machine simply because of the demands of the tasks.

Norm-referenced interpretations are adopted in order to deal with the problem of testing people in areas where objective standards for competence do not exist. Since norm-referenced interpretations are comparisons among persons, the tests must be able to detect differences among them. If a test were so hard that nobody got more than one or two items right, or so easy that no one got more than one or two wrong, there would be no meaningful differences to interpret. From the standpoint of identifying valid differences, it is preferable to have a test where some people get the items almost all right, some get them almost all wrong, and many people get them approximately half right.

One the other hand, tests that identify large differences among learners may produce serious morale problems. It is as if test takers understand criterion-referenced testing implicitly and assume that all tests are criterion-referenced. They do not appreciate that test makers must write difficult items in order to make comparisons among learners. So when they get fewer than 85% correct, they believe they have failed and that they were badly served by their educators. Suggesting that learners assess their performance by comparing themselves to others is usually not helpful because it creates competition among learners which in turn lowers morale.

Although there is no simple solution to this dilemma, there is a worthwhile procedure. First, when there is conflict between pursuing the most accurate assessment of learners and main-taining morale, it is preferable to err on the side of maintaining morale by using relatively easier items. Second, explain that learners should not expect to get the same percentage correct on all tests because some material is more complex and must be dealt with at higher levels. Third, focus learners on identifying where they were relatively more and less successful by asking them to respond to questions such as Were there content areas where you seemed to do better or worse? Were there types of questions where you performed well and not so well? Did you do as well at recalling facts and terms as you did at solving problems or organizing information into an essay? Is this unusual for you? Would it be worthwhile to look at a book on critical thinking, study skills, or test-taking skills?

This set of questions illustrates an important point about test interpretations in informal assessment. Regardless of whether interpretations are criterion- or norm-referenced, a test score is really only a hypothesis about a learner. Therefore, never make a decision about a person on the basis of a single test score. To understand a test taker's strengths, weaknesses, and special characteristics, many sources of information are needed. Understanding is useful to the extent that it leads to improved learning. This point should be made clear to learners whenever they are given interpretations of their test performances.

This approach to interpreting test results does deemphasize the comparisons among learners that are the basis for norm-referenced interpretations. Such comparisons are given more emphasis in the following section on grading.

GRADING

Grading refers to the practice of using a code to characterize the achievement of individual learners. The grades are usually recorded as letters and serve as a permanent evaluation of how well or poorly the learners performed. Many learners dislike being graded because it reduces the great variety of all they do to a single letter. As a condensed summary of a person's performance, grading is neither a substitute for the more individualized test feedback describe above, nor can it be a routine part of adult education. For example, there is likely to be no reason to grade people in a religious education program. If the learners have their own opinions of what they learned, and no one has proposed excommunicating learners who fall below a cutoff score, the grades would be superfluous. On the other hand, there are times when grades are useful. Typically, these are times when someone outside the educational program has an interest in how well learners have achieved. If decisions will be made about the jobs and privileges of learners based wholly or in part on their grades, then every effort should be made to ensure the grading process is sound.

It is useful to begin an analysis of grading with a reminder that grading may be either criterion-referenced or norm-referenced, and that procedures will vary according to which of these systems is used. The examples that follow refer to A, B, C, D, and F to designate the highest to lowest grades because these letters are so widely used. Systems that use other grading codes such as high pass, pass, low pass, and even pass/fail operate analogously.

Criterion-Referenced Grading

Criterion-referenced grading is what most people grow up with. Elementary school tests are usually graded as percent correct so if a child gets 9 out of 10 items correct, he or she gets 90% for the test. At the end of the term the percentages are averaged. If the average is 90% or higher, an A is recorded as the child's grade. If the average is between 80 and 89% inclusive, the child gets a B, and so on for the Cs and Ds. Any average under 60% is an F. (Occasionally, both the average and the letter grade are recorded.) This system is so widespread that many adults have accepted it as the standard for grading practices.

Most people are almost as familiar with criterion-referenced pass/fail grading. This is the system used for granting driver's licenses or certifications for lifeguarding. Cutoff scores are set before the test is taken, and a pass or fail grade is given depending on whether or not the cutoff is exceeded.

Criterion-referenced grading is relatively easy to understand and conduct. It works well in terms of being fair to all learners when learning goals involve mastery of relatively small amounts of objective material such as arithmetic calculations, spelling from short lists of words, or other material where standards for virtual mastery are known and attainable. A source of unfairness can develop if grades are based on tests made by different educators. If one educator makes up long division tests with divisors like 27 and 43, but another educator favors divisors like 11 and 25, the grades from the two educators are really not comparable. Fortunately, this problem does not arise on public tests such as the driver's examination and the lifeguard test because they are made by committees that assure comparability.

Criterion-referenced grading is appropriate for the situations specified above. It is a serious mistake to use it in other situations. Norm-referenced grading is necessary when learning goals involve abstract thought and where there simply are no formal, objective, or shared standards for judging achievement. For example, when a learner takes Elizabethan poetry, the instructor has no handbook to consult in determining which students have written A-level essays, B-level essays, and so on down the line. As a result different instructors may assign different numbers of As, Bs, and so forth on the misperception that they can or should develop a sense of what constitute valid standards. The classic example is the instructor who announces that it is hard to get an A in his class, implying that his standards are rightfully more rigorous than the standards of others.

Norm-Referenced Grading

Norm-referenced grading can and should be used when objective shared standards do not exist because norm-referenced grading uses a curve to substitute for objective standards. Therefore, this section begins with a review of the curving process, but two misconceptions must be clarified at the outset. First, despite its name, grading on a curve does not refer to grading on the normal curve. That practice, which assigns a C to approximately 70% of the learners, has been effectively discarded. Second, grading on a curve is not a matter of adding points to each person's percentage of correct answers in order to adjust for unexpectedly low grades on an individual test.

Grading on a curve is a fair method, perhaps the fairest method, for assigning grades when objective standards of successful learning are not available. It is a method for developing and applying comparable, and sharable standards for grading learners even when they are in different classes with different educators. But reaching consensus on the standards can be complicated, as the following example illustrates. Two educators may be leading comparable classes but giving very different tests. One may give several short objective tests that stress knowledge level outcomes. The other may use only one or two lengthy tests that combine objective with essay questions and emphasize knowledge, application, and synthesis outcomes equally.

At first glance it seems impossible to specify shared standards for achievement in these classes because the tests are so different. However, standards for even large institutions are possible if these two conditions exist within the institution. First, the learners in all classes work about equally hard. Second, the learners in all classes are about equally capable. If these two conditions exist, the educators can agree to define "A" work as the level achieved by some specified percent of the learners at the top of each class; it might be the top 30%. The other grades can be defined analogously. For example, "B" work could be the level achieved by the next 30%, 40%, or whatever the educators decide.

In order to ensure that the curving process is fair to all, educators must be prepared to do some fine tuning. They must keep records of how different classes performed on their tests from year to year. When a particular class does relatively better or worse than other classes, the grades for that class should be adjusted accordingly.

Learners who are unfamiliar with this approach may express concern. They can be reassured with a reminder of the example of the two educators who gave different types of tests. If those educators did not curve their tests, they would have to use percent correct as the basis for the grades. The learners who take the more difficult test, probably the one that includes questions at the application and analysis levels, will get lower grades not because they learned less, but because the test was more challenging. By compensating for such differences in test difficulty, curving is a means for achieving fairness in grading.

There is no one procedure for curving test scores to assign grades. The procedure that is described here is relatively simple, requires no statistical knowledge, and is suitable in most educational settings.

As soon as individual tests have been scored the scores should be given a grade based on a curve, and the grade should be part of test feedback. In order to give learners a clear idea of how they are doing throughout the learning program, it is helpful to give numerical grades which can be averaged at the end of the learning program to yield a letter grade. The process of getting from scores to numerical grades is detailed below.

Second, since grades should be more of a reflection of learning than of the standards of the educator assigning them, they should be assigned according to some objective system. One of the most defensible systems is for the educators at an institution to reach a consensus regarding what percent of learners would receive As, Bs, Cs, and Ds under normal circumstances. The consensus would be a guideline intended to inform, not replace, professional judgment when individual educators assign grades.

When educators at an institution have not formally agreed upon a distribution of letter grades, individual educators can request from the office in charge of record keeping the number of As, Bs and all other letter grades actually recorded at the institution in the last 2 or 3 years; this is the de facto consensus of educators for the appropriate distribution of grades at most institutions. If 30% of the learners at the institution have been getting As, individual educators would want to assign approximately 30% As, and so on for the other letter grades.

This procedure is fair because it neutralizes the individual educator's bias toward assigning high or low grades. What is unfair is for educators to routinely assigning high or low grades in the absence of clear objective evidence that their learners are achieving more or less than the learners in other classes. Assigning higher grades than other educators, penalizes the learners in other classes when all learners are compared on measures such as grade point average and class rank. Similarly, assigning lower grades, penalizes the learners in one's own class. In fact, educators have an obligation to know what grades are given at their institutions so they can bring their grades in line with the rest of the faculty to avoid inadvertently favoring some learners at the expense of others.

The curving process begins with ranking the scores from a test from highest to lowest. The second step is to count down from the top a predetermined number of As. Next, count down the Bs and other letter grades and so on for the remaining letter grades. The process works best for groups of 30 or more, and probably should not be used with fewer than 15 learners. Figure 4.1 illustrates a list of raw scores that are curved in an institution where the grades are usually distributed as 30% A, 30% B, 30% C, 5% D and 5% F.

Thirty percent of the 30 scores is 9 so the highest 9 scores get an A. However, the 9th score is a 55 and so is the 10th which is followed by a gap of 5 scores. Therefore, the first 10 would be given As. The distribution had called for 30 percent or 9 Bs, but in this case only the next 8 scores will be Bs because a score had been added to the As. The 18th score is 42, which is the lowest B. Note that it is hardly different from the 41 that is a C. The closeness calls for an adjustment that is mentioned below. Since there are to be 9 Cs, 30 is the lowest C. Five percent of 30 is 1.5 so it is not possible to have exactly the number of Ds and Fs specified by the distribution. Clearly, the 29s must get the same grade of D. The two point drop to the 27 is not large. In deciding if it is large enough to warrant a failing grade, the educator would examine the range of scores for the other grades. There was a 10 point difference between the highest and lowest A; a 13 point difference between the lowest B and lowest A; and a 12 point difference between the lowest C and lowest B. It would seem inappropriate to have only a two point difference between the highest D and the only F. In this case the judgment of the educator is that the 27 becomes a D, and no one fails despite the fact that the guidelines indicate that 5% of learners normally fail.

When there is a gap between the lowest score for one letter grade and highest score for the next lower letter grade, as there

The following raw scores (indicating the number of correct responses regardless of the number of items on the test) are curved in an institution where the grades are usually distributed as 30% A, 30% B, 30% C, 5% D, and 5% F.

Raw Score	Letter Grade	Numerical Grade
65	A	99
65	A	99
63	A	98
62	A	97
59	A	94
57	A	92
56	A	91
55	A	90
55	A	90
55	A	90
50	B	86
49	B	85
48	B	84
47	B	84
46	B	83
44	B	82
43	B	81
42	B	80
41	C	79
40	C	78
39	C	77
38	C	77
37	C	76
36	C	75
32	C	72
31	C	71
30	C	70
29	D	69
29	D	69
27	D	67

Figure 4.1 Procedures for Curving Grades

was between the lowest A and highest B in this example, all the As might be given the same grade such as a 95 or distinctions might be made among them.

When there are no gaps and/or gaps within letter grades, and this is the more common occurrence, it is advisable that grades be apportioned within the traditional 10-point range for a letter grade. In this example, among the As, 55 gets a grade of 90 and 64 gets 99. For every point above 55 on the score, there is rise of one point above 90 for the grade. No calculations are needed. However, for the Bs it is more complicated. The score of 42 gets a grade of 80, which is the lowest grade in the B range. The range from the lowest B 42, to the highest B, 54, is 13 points when both the 42 and the 54 are included. Divide 10 by 13 to get .77. For every point above 42 up to 54, multiply by .77 and add to 80. Fifty is 8 points above 42, and 8 times .77 equals 6. The grade for a score of 50 is 86. The process is repeated for each letter grade.

The apportioning of grades is not a return to grading on a percent correct basis. It is a way of indicating to learners whether they scored high or low within a letter grade range as well as a way of having numerical grades that can be readily averaged and converted to letter grades at the end of the learning program.

When essays have been scored analytically, each one gets a total number of points. Those points can be curved as outlined above, or they can be added to the points for the objective items on the same test and the sum of the points can be curved. When essays have been scored holistically, the groups of comparable quality are assigned the same score. For example, if the essay question were 20% of a test with a total of 100 points, the best essays might all be given 20 points and each succeeding group be given a score two points lower because 2 out of 20 points is a 10% or traditional letter grade difference. Those scores could then be treated just like the scores from analytical scoring. They could be curved directly as if they were a single test or they could be added to other point totals and the sum could be curved.

An important aspect of grading is calculating a summary

letter grade from the grades on various tests and assignments. A full account of the topic is surprisingly complex and can be found in Gronlund and Linn (1990). However, when educators have grades on criterion-referenced tests that are percentage equivalents (i.e., 19 correct out of 20 = 95) and/or grades that have been curved, they are usually justified in simply calculating the arithmetic average for each learner and then converting the averages into letter grades. Usually averages between 90 and 100 are converted to As, averages between 80 and 89 are converted to Bs, and so forth. Other methods for converting averages to letter grades can be equally useful depending on local circumstances.

Generally, it is less work and less confusing to give all individual grade assignments the same weight in calculating a learner's average. If an educator adopts two learning objectives and one is twice as important as the other is, one strategy is to include the grade of the more important objective twice in calculating the average. However, it is usually preferable to test the more important objective twice, test the less important objective only once, and calculate the average of the three tests. This second option is preferable because it enables the educator to assess the more important objective in more detail and to assess it from different perspectives. For example, by using an essay test and an objective test, the educator could assess learners at the synthesis level with the essay and at the more basic knowledge and comprehension levels with the objective test. Using two tests for the more important objective also sends the clearest message to the learners about the relative importance of the objectives.

There will be times when grades on some test or assignment must be weighted more than others will. In those cases keep the weighting simple so that learners can readily understand it. Avoid situations where one test counts 3.5 times as much as another or where one test counts 50%, a second test counts 35% and a third test counts 15%. Such arrangements often lead to clerical errors on the educator's part. Even worse, they confuse the learners to the point where they distrust the process and the educator. Of course, their distrust quickly shows up as lowered morale and lowered motivation to learn. When grades are given different weights, keep to arrangements where one test carries two or three times the weight of another.

Learners Grading Learners

Peer assessment can be an important part of a total assessment program, but it can complicate grading. It is clear that when one learner examines the work of another, comments on its strengths and weaknesses, makes suggestions for improvement, and so forth, both learners are likely to profit. Recognizing that this type of peer assessment can improve learning, we might ask if learners should take the next step and participate in assigning actual grades or scores that are converted into grades. There is little concern with peers scoring criterion-referenced tests because scoring tests such as a spelling test can be scored perfectly objectively. For example, having learners correct each other's tests is simply a matter of convenience for the teacher that is acceptable as long as it is done honestly and with due consideration to the confidentiality of the learners. The question pertains to norm-referenced grading where one learner would need to judge the quality of the work produced by another learner. For example, an educator could require everyone in a group to write a report, and then divide the group into subgroups of two or more. All the members of one subgroup would meet to read, comment on, and use detailed instructions from the educator to assign a single score on a five-point rating scale to each report written by the members of a different subgroup. The educator could then curve the scores in order to arrive at a grade for each learner.

There are at least four reasons to think that peers should *not* assign scores to one another. First, even when learners have considerable skill in identifying strengths and weakness in a peer's work, there is no assurance that they have the training, experience, or objectivity to score or grade accurately. Second, learners will recognize the possibilities for inaccuracies, lose faith in the validity of their grades, and probably experience a drop in morale. Third, scoring and grading each other's work can damage relationships among learners. Fourth, learners are apt to perceive the educator as shirking his or her responsibility to them. Although the weight of the argument is that learners not assign scores or grades to one another, there is one situation where this injunction does not hold. It is described in Chapter 7 and pertains to a system for having learners grade one another for their contributions to group work.

Gaining Acceptance of Norm-Referenced Grading

To be effective, all grading systems need to be accepted by the learners. An educator should make whatever modifications necessary to have the system accepted without misrepresenting the achievement of learners. One of the easiest ways to make curving acceptable is to add the stipulation that no one will receive a numerical grade lower than what he or she would receive at that institution based on his or her percentage of correct answers. At most institutions this would mean that if a person had 90% of the items correct, that person would get at least an A (Or A– if a +/– system is used at the institution.) regardless of how many people score higher. In fact, this provision rarely comes into play if item difficulty is great enough to measure valid differences among learners. Nonetheless, it placates anxious learners, and it has the additional benefit of taking attention away from the competitive side of curving because everyone can get a good grade simply on the basis of his or her own good work.

IDENTIFYING SKILL DEFICIENCIES

The interpretations discussed so far, including grading, pertain to the achievement of learners. Here the discussion turns to interpretations regarding the difficulties that an individual learner may have.

When a test is written directly from the three-level outline for the test, the items on the test are grouped according to learning objectives. Most often the first group of items are the knowledge level material for the first content area. This group is followed by the higher level items for the first content area. The knowledge level items for the second content area are next, and so on through the test. Therefore, wherever an educator finds a concentration of wrong answers, there is likely to be a content or thinking skill (the levels in the cognitive domain represent different thinking skills) in need of remediation.

In fact one example of identifying skill deficiencies was presented earlier in this chapter under the discussion of providing feedback on essay questions. Here is an example from mathematics:

$$
\begin{array}{ccc}
19 & 22 & 33 \\
\underline{12} & \underline{-19} & \underline{-15} \\
31 & 13 & 28 \\
\end{array}
$$

It seems that this learner has an incomplete understanding of regrouping. He or she is not reducing the 10s column after transferring 10 to the units column. Having identified the skill deficiency, the educator will quickly get this learner back on track.

As simple as this example is, it illustrates the point that learners do have skill deficiencies that can be detected if educators will invest the time to find them. More desirable than having the educator identify deficiencies is having each learner write a self-assessment of the results of his or her test. Learners should be able to indicate whether their missed items were spread evenly throughout the test or concentrated at specific content areas or levels of cognition. They can also suggest methods to remediate their deficiencies and to eliminate similar problems in the future. This is also the time to identify better test study/ learning activities as well as better test preparation and test taking skills. When learners can collaborate in helping one another analyze the results of their tests, the impact can be doubly effective.

ASSESSING LEARNING ACTIVITIES

Evaluating learning activities has much in common with evaluating the performance of individual learners. Instead of looking for content areas and skills where an individual learner had trouble, the educator looks for content areas and skills where the group had trouble. Looking for such areas can be terribly time-consuming, but computing technology is making it easier. When learners answer on computer scan sheets, computers not only score the tests but print out the percentage of test takers answering each item correctly and incorrectly. An educator who has such a printout can see at a glance where the group as a whole had trouble. If there were trouble spots, steps would be provided to remediate those problems before going on. Equally important, the learning activities associated with those trouble spots would be recognized as inadequate and modified before being used in the future. Educators would do well to consult with learners about how to improve those learning activities. Their suggestions might even prevent similar instructional errors in subsequent learning activities.

ASSESSING THE TEST

There are at least three major approaches to assessing an informal test. The first approach, assessing tests before administering them, has been mentioned in Chapter 3. They are really critiques to ensure that all the principles of good test construction have been observed. Ideally, the critiques would be done by educators other than the test maker(s) in order to maximize the objectivity of the critique.

Technical Considerations for Criterion-Referenced Tests

The second approach is a technical analysis of the individual test items. The distinguishing aspect of assessing criterion-referenced tests is based on the opportunity to use the same test as a pretest and a posttest. When the posttest has been scored, the performance of each learner can be charted for each item on the pre and posttest versions. The perfect item is one than nobody answered correctly on the pretest and everybody answered correctly on the posttest. It surely would be saved in the educator's test item pool. Of course, the perfect item would have been associated with successful learning activities and behaviors on the part of the learner, indicating that they should also be continued.

Where items diverge from perfection—learners are hardly more likely to answer correctly on the posttest—learning activities must be considered unsatisfactory. The educator should look for activities that have greater impact on learners. One good source of information on selecting high impact learning activities is Harris (1989).

Technical Considerations for Norm-Referenced Tests

The analysis of norm-referenced tests is a simple matter if the test has been scored by a computer software package designed for the task. Such packages compare how high and low achievers performed on each item. The usual process begins by identifying a high achieving group such as the people who scored in the top 10% of those taking the test and a corresponding low achieving group which in this case would be the people who scored in the bottom 10%. The next step is to find how many people in the bottom group answered the first item correctly and subtract that from the number of people in the top group who answered it correctly. The expectation, and desired result, is that the number will be positive indicating that the people who did well on the test as a whole also did well on this individual item, in which case nothing need be done.

As the number gets closer to 0, the item is said to be doing a less effective job of separating the more knowledgeable from the less knowledgeable learners, indicating that it should be examined. Perhaps it is a confusing item and everyone is just guessing at the answer. Possibly it is so hard nobody can get it right or so easy nobody can get it wrong. The educator may want to revise it before returning it to the item pool.

If the learners in the bottom are more likely to answer correctly than the ones in the top, the item definitely would have to be examined. It may contain a flaw that needs to be removed before it is used again. It may be that the wrong answer had been keyed into the computer. A third possibility is that a subtle point during a learning activity gave a misconception to the more attentive learners. Very rarely would this unexpected result occur by chance with a basically good item.

Another important calculation the software performs is dividing the number of people who answer correctly by the number of people taking the test. This gives an overall indication of how difficult the test item is for the group. As mentioned above, for the purpose of accurately identifying the more from the less knowledgeable learners, the items need to be fairly difficult. If everyone got all the items correct, no differentiation would exist among the test takers. Similarly, no differentiation would be made if everyone got all the items wrong.

A common recommendation is that the average learner should "know" the answers for one-half of the items of an objective test. In practice this is not quite the same as 50% correct because it is possible to guess correctly a sizeable portion of the select items. Therefore, the following recommendation is made: The average learner should score halfway between what a person would get correct simply by guessing (knowing none of the answers) and 100% correct (knowing all or almost all the answers). On a true/false test, where a person would guess right half the time, the recommendation is for $1/2(50\% + 100\%) =$ 75% correct. For a multiple-choice test where there are always four options, a person would guess 25% of the answers so the calculation is $1/2(25\% + 100\%) = 62.5\%$.

Sometimes adult learners have difficulty accepting 62.5% correct as acceptable performance. It is as if somewhere in elementary school they formed an unbreakable habit of thinking that 90% correct is an A and anything lower than 85% is unacceptable. When this is the mind set of the learners it is hardly worth the effort of trying to change their thinking. They don't

want to be told about the difference between norm- and criterion-referenced testing. They will not accept the fact that half
the doctors graduate in the bottom half of their medical school
class. Learners want to get 90% correct.

Unfortunately, it sometimes happens that in order to have
test takers answering approximately 90% correct, it is necessary
to increase the proportion of lower level (involving simply memory) items. Since it is better to maintain high morale than technically perfect assessment, educators should consider compro-
mising the recommendation regarding the percentage that the
average learner should get correct. One acceptable compromise
is to design a technically correct test and then add lower level
items. This way learners can score high in terms of percentage
and they still are challenged by an appropriate array of higher
levels items. (Hopefully they won't complain that the tests are
too long.)

The Learners Assess the Test

The third approach to assessing tests is one very few educators use—asking the learners to assess their tests. Nonetheless, it is a good practice. It does seem wise to structure their
assessments in order to get more than off-the-cuff comments
such as, "It was okay; too hard; too long; not too long; not long
enough;" and so forth. One solution is to give the learners a
questionnaire to fill out and return anonymously. Sample items
could be:

• Did you have a clear idea of what would be on the test when
  you were studying for it? If not, why not?
• Did the test cover the important aspects of what we have been
  learning? If not what was left out?
• What about the test made it hard for you to do your best?
• What did you think was best and worst about the test?
• How could the test be more like the demands of your job?

This kind of investigation not only helps the educator improve the tests but it sets the learners to thinking about assess-

ment—a step which is surely a prerequisite to becoming competent critics of their own work.

LOOKING BEYOND TRADITIONAL TESTS

Traditional paper and pencil tests do have a significant role in adult education. They focus learners on important objectives, motivate learners to study effectively, and enable educators to accurately assess competence. Unfortunately, even when every effort has been made to upgrade tests, they have limitations that are reflected in charges such as the following:

- They obscure many talents such as creativity and curiosity.
- They encourage passivity in learners.
- They ignore individual learning/performance styles.
- They emphasize "classroom" activities at the expense of performing the tasks of real life.

Given that these charges are to a certain extent legitimate, reliance on paper and pencil testing for all summative assessment would be a mistake. Educators should always be looking to incorporate additional methods into their assessment programs. The next chapter discusses assessment methods that are designed to overcome the limitations of paper and pencil testing mentioned above.

CHAPTER 5

Achieving Authenticity
in Performance Assessments

Educators have turned to performance assessments in an effort to overcome some of the limitations of teacher-centered paper and pencil assessment. Specifically, they look to performance assessments to

- Emphasize complex real-life tasks.
- Accommodate individual learning/performance styles.
- Give learners a greater say in how they are assessed.
- Uncover talents such as creativity and curiosity.
- Encourage activity in learners, especially in selecting learning goals.

THE NATURE OF
PERFORMANCE ASSESSMENTS

Performance assessments involve learners in completing a task whereas paper and pencil tests are more likely to require learners to display what they know about the task. But, the dividing line between traditional paper and pencil testing and performance assessment is anything but sharp. It is probably best to think of them as ends of a continuum with certain types of assessment right in the middle. Essay tests were treated as part of the paper and pencil assessment arsenal, not because people actually use paper and pencils when they write essays, but because restricted form essays are so often used to measure what people know about particular topics. For example, asking learners to compare the roles of teachers and learners in teacher-centered and learner-centered education requires them to display what they know about these two styles of education so they are involved in traditional paper and pencil assessment. On the other hand, test takers who are asked to write an unstructured essay that includes synthesizing original designs for teacher-centered and learner-centered activities for a given content are demonstrating their ability to perform a real-life task, and so they might be said to be involved in performance assessment. Learners who are asked to design and carry out a teacher-centered and a learner-centered activity for specified content are unquestionably involved in performance assessment. The more a learner is assessed for completing a "real-life" task the more likely it will be considered a performance assessment.

Performances may vary considerably in complexity—they could be as simple as spelling a word correctly. More often they are of some intermediate level such as "rescuing" from a swimming pool a lifeguard who is acting as though he is drowning, parking an 18-wheel truck between orange and white cones, or writing a book review. They can be as complicated as conducting an orchestra or completing biochemical research as part of a doctoral dissertation. As implied in the examples above, the performances may also vary considerably in realism. For example, in a course on public speaking, the learners may simply write a speech, give the speech in front of classmates, or give the speech to a formal audience at a community gathering. Similarly, performance assessments are conducted in many media and utilize multiple sensory modes. Computer simulations will likely become a common means of conducting performance assessments because of their potential for involving multiple senses in a dynamic fashion. For example, firefighters in training might use a computer program to simulate giving first aid to burn victims. One part of the promise of performance assessments is that they are more fair to learners because they assess learners on the tasks they are preparing to perform in the real world (Wislock, 1993).

DECIDING WHEN TO USE PERFORMANCE ASSESSMENTS

Throughout the discipline of education there is currently a great deal of enthusiasm for performance assessments. It is as if educators believe that in assessing learners on the performance of real-life tasks they have finally got assessment right. Although performance assessment is neither new nor a panacea, it is an important part of assessment that has probably been underutilized in the recent past. Most likely learners will be best served by educators who blend paper and pencil assessment with performance assessment in varying proportions to address the learning objectives of given situations.

The planning grid that was introduced in Chapter 3 as a means of planning traditional paper and pencil tests is just as useful in planning performance assessments and in blending these two into an assessment package. The planning grid was used to specify the content and the cognitive levels at which the learners would study and be assessed. The three-level outline was used to add the specific learning outcomes—what the learners would do to demonstrate achievement. Of course the outcomes can be written to specify either test taking or task performance. An illustration of how performance assessments are blended into assessment planning follows.

The three-level outline on parenting presented in Figure 3.3 contains only the outcomes of knowing. An educator might check the outline and recognize that a learner could know the answers to all the questions on the test and still perform poorly as a parent. The measures of knowing provide a limited and possibly misleading indication of a person's accomplishments. In fact, it seems wise to add specific learning outcomes that are stated as performance assessments. In this case, they might be added to the measurement of the application for both Principles of Discipline and Effective Communication. In fact, the underlined portions of Figure 5.1 have been added to Figure 3.3 as performance outcomes designed to measure applications for those two content areas. These outcomes call for a professional

I. Causes of Misbehavior
   A. Knowledge
      1. Matches terms to definitions
      2. Recognizes correct statements regarding causes of misbehavior
   B. Analysis
      1. Selects correct causes of misbehavior in scenarios
II. Principles of Discipline
   A. Comprehension
      1. Explains principles in own words
   B. Application
      1. Recommends disciplinary action for specified offenses
      2. Administers discipline to own child in own home
III. Effective Communication
   A. Knowledge
      1. Defines terms
      2. Matches terms to definitions
   B. Application
      1. Recommends responses to child's statements
      2. Responds to own child's statements in observation room
   C. Evaluation
      1. Assesses statements by parents to children in scenarios

Figure 5.1 Performance Outcomes (underlined) Added to Test Outline for Parenting Education (Figure 3.3)

to observe and rate the learner as he or she interacts with children. The observations could take place through a one-way glass window to a play room, on a field trip, or during a weekend visit by the professional to the learner's home.

Figure 5.1 demonstrates that there is no formal difficulty incorporating performance assessments into the planning process described in Chapter 3. In fact, the entire assessment could be composed of task performance. Normally, the challenge is to strike the right balance between assessing what a person knows and how a person performs because performance assessments have limitations as well as strengths just as traditional paper and pencil tests do.

In areas where performance is largely mental as it is in

communicating with children, observing that a person has performed poorly on a task does not pinpoint the nature of the
person's difficulty. For example, if a parent imposes inappropriate consequences for misbehavior, the observer would need additional information to determine why the parent chose the inappropriate consequences. A set of multiple-choice items might
be able to identify gaps in the learners knowledge base that need
filling. A related problem is that since performance assessments
are so time-consuming it is difficult to use them to assess all that
a learner may be expected to have acquired. He or she may have
done very well during a performance despite having great short-
comings in other areas that were not addressed. For example, if
the parent communicated well on a topic such as the child's sadness, but, within the allotted time, was not challenged by a discussion of the child's anger, the performance assessment might
overestimate his or her capability to communicate whereas a set
of multiple-choice questions might reveal that the learner com-
prehends the principles for communicating on matters involving
fear, sadness, and joy, but not anger.

It seems to make sense to plan assessments to take advantage of the strengths of both types of assessments. In general, a
comprehensive assessment plan would include paper and pencil
testing to determine what a learner does and does not know
about the individual topics in a learning program and performance assessments to assess the most complex achievements expected of the learners in the learning program.

PERFORMANCE ASSESSMENT
CHARACTERISTICS

A short while ago, some options were suggested for observing and assessing the performance of learners in a course on
parenting. It was suggested that "the observations could take
place through a one-way glass window to a play room, on a field
trip, or during a weekend visit by the professional to the family's
home." These observations are arranged in order of increasing
realism and as the realism increases the time required to perform

the observation also increases. Educators are commonly forced
to compromise a desire to use the most realistic task and a desire
to spend as little time as possible completing the assessment.
Although there is no solution to the dilemma, there are two
questions that often help an educator make a choice.

First, how much is the learner likely to learn from performing the more realistic and time-consuming task? An answer to
that question is available to the educators who monitor the re-
actions of their learners to their assessments over a period of
years. When an educator has reason to believe that an assessment will double as a learning activity, then it is appropriate to
choose the realistic task even if it is more time-consuming.

Second, how serious a mistake would it be to misrepresent
a learner's accomplishments on a given assessment? Clearly,
every educator endeavors to be accurate with each assessment.
But in fact, educators often need to minimize assessment time
in order to maximize learning time. That means accepting that
some assessments will be helpful but less than ideal. If a learner
is going to be assessed subsequently, perhaps a less realistic and
less time-consuming assessment is appropriate. If a learner is
being certified for some significant duty such as lifeguarding,
only a realistic performance will due.

Process or Product

In many situations, the distinction between process and
product proves helpful in deciding what to assess. In assessing
someone learning to type (or keyboard), is it preferable to examine the process by observing posture, location of the copy,
positioning of the fingers on the keys, and tendency to look at
the keys, or the product by calculating words per minute cor-
rected for errors?

An educator might very well focus on process for formative
assessment when people are just beginning their learning. Similarly, if a given learner were typing slowly, a focus on the process
would seem appropriate. In both cases, there are reasons to believe that examining the process will identify and ultimately
remedy difficulties and yield improved typing. On the other

hand, assessment of learners at the end of their programs would probably be better focused on the product. All learners have presumably had the opportunity to develop their skills, taking into account their own resources, and then show what they can do. This is also the case if a learner can produce a desirable product in several different ways or if the process is difficult to observe as it is when a person writes a poem.

Analytic and Holistic Scoring

A performance can be viewed as a compilation of discrete parts or as a unit. Scoring procedures differ according to how the performance is viewed. Analytic scoring refers to rating the individual aspects of the performance whereas holistic scoring refers to rating the performance as a whole. Analytic scoring would be seriously considered whenever a process or product can be readily apportioned into observable components. Giving a speech is an example of a process that can be properly assessed in terms of the individual components such as voice, nonverbal communication, communication aids, organization, and logic. Similarly, a painting could be scored for color, perspective, match of medium to theme, and so forth. Holistic scoring is generally more suitable in situations where it is difficult to observe discrete components of a performance or if there were several ways to produce a satisfactory product. A poem in a writing class, and an entree for a culinary course are examples of learning products that might be rated holistically.

It must to be noted that any process or product that can be rated analytically can also be rated holistically. For example, giving a speech might be more properly assessed in terms of the overall impact rather than the individual aspects of the speech. So an educator may choose between analytic and holistic ratings on the basis of the purpose of the assessment. If a given assessment were more formative and interest were on identifying strengths and weakness, the analytic ratings of voice, nonverbal communication, communication aids, organization, logic, and the like would seem to be a better choice. If the assessment were more summative, as in giving an award in a public speaking contest, the holistic ratings would be superior. Of course, there is nothing to prevent an educator from using a combination of the two rating systems.

MEASUREMENT INSTRUMENTS

Educators use rating scales and similar instruments to help them score performances adequately, objectively, reliably, and validly. Most often they must develop on their own or modify existing instruments in order to have instruments appropriate for their individual situations. There are several matters to consider in developing an instrument beginning with the form of the instrument.

Rating Scales

Rating scales can be devised for either analytic or holistic use. A rating scale for holistic use is simply a set of points representing different levels of quality. It is like grading a speech A, B, C, D, or F. A rating scale for analytic use contains a separate set of points for each aspect of the performance that is perceived to be important and readily observable. In the example of the learner who is giving a speech, the core of an analytic rating scale was suggested in listing voice, nonverbal communication, communication aids, organization, and logic as the aspects of the speech that could be rated. The scale would list each of them and provide space to record how well the learner performed on each of these aspects of the performance. An example of a rating scale in found in Figure 5.2.

In this case the points on the scale have been defined in terms of the concept average. In some situations it is possible to use more objective quantitative descriptions of the points. For example, if the task were to back a truck between cones set 12 feet apart, a driver might receive a rating of 3 for knocking over no cones, 2 for knocking over 1–2 cones, and 1 for 3 or more cones.

Rate the speaker on each dimension. Please use the following key.				
1	2	3	4	5
Far Below Average	Below Average	About Average	Above Average	Far Above Average
VOICE		1 2 3 4 5		
NONVERBAL COMMUNICATION		1 2 3 4 5		
COMMUNICATION AIDS		1 2 3 4 5		
ORGANIZATION		1 2 3 4 5		
LOGIC		1 2 3 4 5		

Figure 5.2 Rating Scale for Assessing a Speech

Rubrics

Rubrics are means of refining rating scales. The idea is to provide a detailed description of what each number on the scale represents. An example of a rubric is found in Figure 5.3. It would be used for analytic scoring since it covers five individual aspects of a speech. This example of a rubric for analytic scoring illustrates the advantage of the analytic approach and the advantage of a rubric over a rating scale in helping learners recognize strengths and weaknesses in their work.

Of course, rubrics can also be used in holistic assessment. Each point on the scale would be accompanied by a detailed description.

Benchmarks

Benchmarks are actual samples of the products. They are used to supplement or replace the detailed descriptors found in rubrics. For each numbered point on the rating scale there will be a sample to illustrate what quality of work that point repre-

Assign points on each dimension according to the accompanying descriptors.

VOICE
   0 unintelligible
   1 could be understood with difficulty
   2 could be understood without difficulty
   3 facilitated understanding

NONVERBAL COMMUNICATION
   0 no eye contact or gesturing
   1 minimal eye contact and gesturing
   2 adequate eye contact and appropriate gesturing
   3 eye contact and gestures established rapport with audience

COMMUNICATIONS AIDS
   0 no communications aids
   1 communications aids not helpful
   2 adequate communication aids
   3 attention getting and informative communications aids

ORGANIZATION
   0 no apparent organization
   1 obvious gaps in organization
   2 adequate organization
   3 superior organization clearly presented to audience

LOGIC
   0 multiple serious mistakes in logic
   1 at least one serious logical error
   2 no serious logical errors
   3 compelling logic throughout

Figure 5.3 A Rubric for Rating a Speech

sents. An example of benchmarking is found in Figure 5.4. In this case, parents are asked to frame a reply to a child who has objected to plans to go to grandma's house. The parents are supposed to reflect the child's feelings, and gently but firmly enforce a prior decision to go to grandma's house. The 0 Point comments are benchmarks for failing to reflect feelings and/or failing to gently and firmly enforce the decision. The 3 Point comments are benchmarks for success on each count.

CHILD'S REMARK:
"I don't want to go to grandma's house. It's stupid."

BENCHMARKS FOR PARENT'S REPLY:

0 Points
- Okay, we just won't go.
- You get a really bad spanking for that.

1 Point
- Don't ever say that again.
- Just get in the car and keep quiet.

2 Points
- Going to grandma's house is not that bad.
- Don't worry we won't stay long.

3 Points
- Honey, I'm sorry you don't want to go today. But we told grandma we would visit her so we have to get going.
- We need to go to grandma's. Is there something we could do to make the trip fun?

Figure 5.4 Benchmarks for Assessing Parents' Responses to a Child's Remark

Benchmarks are especially useful for making holistic ratings of nonverbal products. This is sometimes the case because of difficulties in describing various aspects of a product and sometimes because of a need to assess how well a product functions as a whole. Actual handcrafted furniture, photographs of residential landscaping projects, and samples of handwriting (because the concern is the psychomotor skill) could serve as highly effective visual benchmarks.

DEVELOPING ASSESSMENT INSTRUMENTS

Clearly, educators who facilitate a group of learners would be expected to devise scales for use with their learners. On the other hand, they would not necessarily do all the work themselves. As part of their professional activities they would collect instruments from journals, conferences, and colleagues with the expectation that they will adapt those instruments for their own use. In addition, they could collaborate with colleagues to develop instruments and critique one another's work. Collaboration is especially helpful for educators working in the same or closely related institutions with similar learning goals.

On occasion, individuals who are outside the learning program can make valuable contributions to the development of the assessment instruments. They may be content experts, assessment experts, or people who have a stake in how well learners perform after they leave the learning setting, for example, supervisors who are expecting improved job performance at the conclusion of the leaning/training session. Having stakeholders contribute to the development of the instruments will direct and motivate both educators and learners to pursue important outcomes as well as appropriate levels of accomplishment.

Learner's should be involved as much as possible in developing instruments. They should contribute to developing the instruments even before they begin their learning activities as a way of identifying important learning outcomes and directing their learning behaviors toward those outcomes. The learners should also review the assessment instruments in the midst of their learning activities as a way to fine-tune the instruments in light of the expertise they have acquired from their learning activities. When learners review assessment instruments, they can simultaneously assess their learning progress, and their learning activities.

USING MEASURING DEVICES

Using rating scales, rubrics, and benchmarks significantly increases the reliability and validity of assessments, especially when raters are trained to use them. The training can be accomplished rather easily. Two or more people rate a set of performances—processes and/or products—independently and then discuss their ratings. The discussions will naturally focus on the differences in ratings. Occasionally, the discussions will lead to changes in the instruments. At other times, individual raters will clarify misconceptions, develop shared standards, and gradually become more consistent in their ratings.

For reasons of economy, most ratings of learners are made by a single educator. However, the more important the assessment, the more appropriate it is to have multiple raters assess each learner. When two or more raters assess a single learner, discrepancies in the ratings can be a considerable problem. Simple averaging saves time and it has the advantage of being objective. However, negotiating may be preferable because discrepancies are often the result of one rater overlooking an aspect of what is being rated rather than the result of a difference of opinion; so negotiation may yield more accurate scores.

Outside raters are sometimes needed for their expertise. One example is a doctoral dissertation committee that includes a faculty member from another university whose function is to provide expertise that is not available at the university where the candidate is earning the degree. Similarly, a psychologist who is using a learning contract to develop skills in personality testing that the supervisor doesn't possess would want to have his or her accomplishments assessed by an outside expert. Sometimes, each person in a continuing education class will undertake a learning contract. The educator who is leading the class may find that he or she is not sufficiently informed to fully assess each contract, and request that the learners with such contracts obtain an outside assessment in addition to his or her own assessment.

Stakeholders are sometimes valuable as outside assessors. In a situation where learners are being prepared for specific workplace tasks, it makes sense for the people who will supervise those tasks to perform some of the assessments, particularly formative assessments. The feedback they supply can ensure that learners and potential supervisors will be concentrating on the same goals.

The use of outside raters does introduce complications. When they are rating people that they know, their ratings may be influenced by their feelings for the people. Similarly, if they have not been trained to use particular instruments, they may have idiosyncratic notions of what constitutes quality performance. Both of these problems can be reduced by using rubric and benchmarks.

One of the most helpful uses of assessment instruments is for learners to rate their own work and the work of their peers. Learner ratings are especially effective and efficient as formative evaluation as long as they have been trained to use the instruments.

Rating scales, rubrics, and benchmarks are all important means of assessing performances. However, they can be enhanced by providing written comments that learners can use to improve their future performances. Such comments would be similar to comments appended to learners' essays; they would expand on the strengths and weaknesses pointed out in the ratings, provide suggestions for change, and end with encouragement.

One concern is that feedback from peers and outside raters is sometimes overly candid. Educators are wise to train these groups in providing feedback so that ratings and comments are encouraging. Furthermore, educators should review the peer assessments and revise them if necessary. A second concern is that peer ratings can be contaminated by halo effects—the tendency to rate people higher or lower than their performances warrant on the basis of irrelevant factors such as physical appearance or friendship. Detailed rubrics and benchmarks coupled with an explanation of halo effects and their evils are effective preventions.

ASSESSING PERFORMANCE
ASSESSMENT PROGRAMS

Regardless of how much care has been devoted to developing assessment instruments and using them properly, there will be a need for periodic checks of the assessment process with special attention toward combating subjectivity in scoring and maintaining relevance of the assessment for the personal and professional lives of learners.

Subjectivity

Refresher training of the raters is one of the better methods for combating subjectivity. Training would occur at regular intervals with several raters for a given type of performance submitting a random sample of performances along with their actual ratings of those performances. As part of the training, they would then rate the performances submitted by one another. If possible each performance would be rated more than once after being submitted. Finally, each person would receive their original submission accompanied by anonymous ratings produced by fellow trainees. Discrepancies in the ratings could indicate problems and would be examined.

During the examination each trainee might characterize their tendencies. One of the central concerns would be whether his or her ratings are generally high or low compared to the others. A second concern is whether there is an indication that the ratings are based too heavily on only one aspect of a performance. For example, in holistic assessment of speeches, the rater may put too much emphasis on communication aids and not enough or organization or vice versa. It would even be possible to detect tendencies to rate groups (men or women, younger or older people) of learners high or low. Probably, every rater will drift toward idiosyncratic ratings. Fortunately, if they participate in refresher training, these problems can be remedied easily.

The refresher training can be particularly worthwhile for educators who are pursuing the same learning goals in separate locations. Community college faculty concerned with writing skills would profit from sessions not only to validate their ratings of written work but also as a way to maintain standards at their home institutions. Educators who train people to perform

CPR would be able to reorient one another toward standards of competence.

Relevance

Assessment instruments themselves need to be reviewed and updated to make sure that what is rated is important in the world outside the learning program. Stakeholders such as employers are an obvious resource for the review and updating. They have information about changes in the demands of the workplace, and they are usually quite willing to help since they can expect to be beneficiaries of any improvements they can suggest. A somewhat less obvious resource is the pool of learners who have gone through a learning program and tried to build on it. They may be the best resource when learning programs are not conducted for specific employers. They can give information about what employers in general are looking for and they can comment on what they learned in the program that proved to be meaningful. Such comments point an educator toward revising assessments to address the issues that are relevant to their learners.

GRADING

Performance assessments do not have to lead to grades of any sort. However, there are times when educators must submit grades based on performance assessments. In those cases they can use the procedures for grading essays with very little modification. If they had used analytical scoring, they can curve the total scores on individual performances or add them to other point totals before curving. If they used holistic scoring, they can group individual performances on overall quality, assign points to each group, and treat the points just as if they were assigned analytically.

SUMMARY

At the outset of this chapter there was a list of some of the hopes educators have for performance assessments. It seems that the first three on the list have been covered: By definition performance assessments do emphasize real-life tasks. In basing assessment on real-life tasks, there is a shift away from the verbal mode of paper and pencil tests so learners whose styles and strengths are in other modes have a better opportunity to be assessed in terms of what they do best. Finally, the discussions of how and why to involve learners in developing and even using rating instruments make it clear that performance assessments do give learners a significant say in how they are assessed.

But what about uncovering talents and encouraging active learning? In some ways they seem the more compelling reasons for using performance assessments, but they were not addressed in this chapter; however, they are in the forefront of Chapter 6 where managing multiple performance assessments via portfolios is discussed.

CHAPTER 6

Mastering Performance Portfolios

Portfolio assessment probably attracted more attention than any other concept within the field of educational assessment during the 1990s. It is by no means a new idea. In fact it has been one of the mainstays of assessment in areas such as visual arts and language arts for as long as people can remember. What is new is the extension of portfolio assessment to many other areas and the incorporation of techniques to involve learners in assessing their own portfolios. In light of this emphasis on involving learners, portfolio assessment is especially well suited to adult education. Some would even suggest that portfolio assessment is simply an outgrowth of implementing the principles of andragogy, the art and science of helping adults learn (Knowles, 1980).

From the standpoint of educational assessment, a portfolio is a collection of what a learner has produced, and it is organized to demonstrate the progress of the learner toward specified learning objectives. According to this definition the collection could include virtually any type of product. It could be as simple as a set of paper and pencil arithmetic tasks arranged to demonstrate the learner's proficiency. As such it might include

- homework
- workbook exercises
- extra credit assignments
- quizzes
- examinations

This would not be so much a departure from paper and pencil testing as an organization of that testing in order to facilitate an assessment of the learners' progress, deficiencies, and efforts.

At the other end of the spectrum might be a collection of evidence to demonstrate an educator's skills. It might include

- documented preparation for teaching
- description of teaching responsibilities
- statement of philosophy of teaching
- sample lesson plans and teaching materials arranged to illustrate how that philosophy is implemented
- sample assessment systems and materials arranged to illustrate how that philosophy is implemented
- videotaped demonstrations of teaching
- learners' products
- assessments of teaching from supervisors, peers, and learners
- statement of professional development history, goals, and activities

The second example is a departure from paper and pencil testing because it is essentially a collection of performances and because it is learner centered in both planning and assessment. As such it has the capability to uncover and develop talents. In this case, perhaps the educator will display skill and creativity in developing teaching materials with computer technology.

The teaching portfolio also illustrates each of the four aspects of organization for portfolios. First, there should be a statement of the learning goals—the philosophy of teaching serves as that statement here. Second, there is a presentation of learning products to demonstrate the attainment of the goals—in this portfolio the products are the lesson plans, teaching aids and demonstrations of teaching. Third, there is also an assessment of accomplishments, which here is gathered largely from stakeholders who are supervisors and learners. Fourth and finally, there is a statement of future learning goals, which take the form of professional development goals. The statement of future learning goals is particularly important in encouraging active learning because it sets up a subsequent round of learner-centered activities.

Clearly portfolios are not an alternative to the paper and pencil tests or performance assessments described in previous chapters. They are a means of organizing those individual tests and performances in order to assess a learner's overall progress, versatility, and creativity. By virtue of using portfolios to assess versatility and creativity, there can be no single best portfolio assessment system. Instead there are an infinite number of successful adaptations of portfolios to individual situations. Therefore, in preparing to use portfolios, an educator does not learn about a system as was the case in using a planning grid for a paper and pencil test. Rather an educator develops a sense of what kinds of assessment information portfolios can provide and how portfolios can be adapted to particular situations.

ORGANIZING PORTFOLIO ASSESSMENTS

Portfolio assessment clearly has a number of significant advantages over traditional testing. Those advantages materialize to the extent that the portfolios are managed successfully. Although there can not be one single best way of conducting portfolio assessments, there are several guidelines for practitioners. General guidelines for assessment apply, but to a large extent success depends on

- what products will be stored
- how they will be stored
- how they will be rated
- how learners receive feedback
- who makes the decisions about all the above

Each of these matters is addressed below.

Choosing What Will Be Stored

It may be true that any learning product can be stored for portfolio assessment, but storing everything indiscriminately is usually counterproductive because the process becomes excessively time-consuming. Therefore, the recommended practice is to store those learning products that make the portfolio clearly superior to any other way of representing a learner's progress, versatility, creativity, and self-direction. Generally, this means storing performance products that represent the culmination of extensive work such as a chair in a woodworking course, a watercolor in an art class, a poem in a writing seminar, and a filed income tax form in a training program. If space becomes a problem as it would if a number of chairs were stored, some method for representing them is often needed. Photographs of each chair taken from different angles might be suitable.

Portfolios may also involve performance processes that have been reproduced in some fashion. A videotape of a performance would be quite suitable—note that a rating of a performance would be relatively unsatisfactory because it would lack the character of the learner's individual style.

After identifying the learning products to be included, there is the question of making the portfolios illustrative or comprehensive for that type of learning product. Illustrative portfolios contain only a sample of what a learner has produced. The sample could be designed to reveal what is typical of a learner, what is the best of the learner's work, or what progress the learner has made. To avoid confusion, a description of exactly how the contents were sampled should be appended in a conspicuous location. Illustrative portfolios have the obvious advantage of requiring less storage capacity, making it easier to maintain them during lengthy learning programs and even extend them from one learning program to another as would be the case of a learner who is taking an associate's degree in woodworking. In addition, illustrative portfolios are much less time-consuming during summative assessments.

On the other hand, comprehensive portfolios are collections of all that a learner has produced (at least all of the type of learning product relevant for the portfolio). The trade-off is obvious; comprehensive portfolios provide a more detailed account of learning, but they can become burdensome to store and review.

Choosing How Items Will Be Stored

Materials can be stored in any form that leaves the learning products accessible, durable, secure, inexpensive, reproducible, and compact. Paper in folders is still an effective medium and probably the medium of choice for watercolors and similar products. Many items that might have formerly been stored on paper can and should be stored on computer disks. Text and computer graphics can be stored and copied so readily on disk that educators should at least consider them. Videotapes may be a wonderful way to record performances from dance to volleyball and even counseling. They may also prove frustrating if learners have their individual tapes, but must share a single recorder or player. The bottom line is to consider technology as a way to ease the problems of storage.

Rating Portfolios

If the items in a portfolio are the products of learners performing real-life tasks, and this is usually the case, then those products would be assessed according to the procedures outlined in the previous chapter. What is new is the possibility of assessing the portfolio as a whole.

Assessing the portfolio products as a whole does not require any new principles. Most often it simply requires additional rating instruments. The instruments can be either analytic or holistic, and they may be developed by the educator alone or in collaboration with the learners. However, the criteria used for assessing portfolios almost invariably include evidence of (1) learning progress, (2) versatility, (3) creativity, and (4) self-direction.

Learning Progress

One of the primary reasons for using portfolios is to have records of learners' accomplishments that can be the basis for assessing their progress. Educators who wish to assess progress from multiple perspectives can draw on the six categories of educational goals that were introduced in Chapter 2. Perhaps the simplest procedure is to make a recording form using the categories of educational goals as the headings and filling in subheadings that suit the learning program. The six levels of the cognitive domain, which were described in Chapter 3, could serve as a set of subheadings under "Thinking Skills" for most learning programs. A sample form is in Figure 6.1.

Then each time educators review portfolios; they would rate the performance and comment on the progress of the learners regarding those categories. If they were using the form in Figure 6.1, they would begin by assessing thinking skills, under which there are six levels of cognition. For example, they might comment on whether a learner applies skills to novel situations, analyzes the strengths and weakness in his or her own work, synthesizes information from diverse sources, and so on. They would make comparable comments for the other categories.

There are many reasons for keeping records of the progress of individual learners. The records enable educators to characterize the achievements of the learners to stakeholders such as potential employers and to assign grades when administrators require them. One of greatest benefits is that the learners can observe for themselves the progress they have made. When they recognize that they have progressed from the beginning to the middle or the end of a learning program, they get a wonderful boost in self-esteem and motivation to participate in other learning programs.

At another level, a record of the progress of the individuals in a program provides feedback on the effectiveness of the program. Educators can keep a tally of what percentage of learners express satisfaction with their progress as a general indicator of program effectiveness. They can also be very specific. For example, an educator in a program designed to teach workers to write business letters could compare letters written at the beginning and end of the program to determine what percentage of workers changed from writing excessively wordy letters to writing succinct letters. In fact, educators can collect data from portfolios and assess virtually all meaningful aspects of their learning programs. This paragraph barely introduces the concept of using performance assessments to evaluate learning programs. Readers who want a comprehensive account of this and other approaches to assessing learning programs are referred to Vella, Berardinelli, and Burrow (1998) and to Kirkpatrick (1998).

Notes for Conference With _____

Date _____   Subject _____

Thinking Skills: Knowledge, Comprehension, Application, Synthesis, and Evaluation
   Observation:

   Interpretation:

Basic Academic Skills:
   Observation:

   Interpretation:

Discipline-Specific Knowledge:
   Observation:

   Interpretation:

Liberal Arts Values:
   Observation:

   Interpretation:

Work Preparation:
   Observation:

   Interpretation:

Personal Development:
   Observation:

   Interpretation:

Figure 6.1 Form for Recording Conference Notes

Versatility

In certain disciplines, there may appear to be no meaningful distinction between assessing progress and versatility. For example, educators who deal with keyboarding skills or physics may not benefit from considering versatility as a separate issue. On the other hand, educators who are helping adults write poetry or develop counseling skills probably would want to address versatility. They might do so by explaining why versatility is important and develop with them an instrument for assessing versatility. The instrument could be as simple as a question: What forms of poetry can you write successfully? Or what types of clients or client problems can you address competently?

Creativity

Creativity resists definition. However, it is helpful to think of creativity as explaining events and solving problems in new and effective ways. One of the advantages of portfolios over traditional paper and pencil tests is their capability for displaying the products of creative efforts. Traditional testing proceeds by giving a single task to learners and then comparing the learners either to a predetermined standard (criterion referenced) or to other learners (norm referenced). This approach has its place, but it is not effective for assessing the innovations that are a part of creativity. Portfolios, on the other hand, actually encourage learners to be creative by giving them the freedom to attempt different types of tasks in different styles of their own choosing.

Assessing creativity is somewhat more subjective than other types of assessment. The process becomes more reliable when it is based upon a larger number of projects. Therefore, the portfolio as a whole, including the aforementioned capability for illustrating versatility, is particularly suitable for assessing creativity. Similarly, the assessments are more reliable when they are done by groups of people who are themselves open to new ideas.

The actual assessment of creativity cannot be any more teacher centered than the portfolio development without stifling the creative efforts of the learners. Learners should be encouraged to read about creativity and develop a set of criteria, possibly rubrics, for assessing creativity.

Self-direction

Self-direction is like creativity in being difficult to define and observe directly. What may be different is that learners are inclined to think about being or becoming more creative. They seem less inclined to consciously think about self-direction unless an educator brings the concept to their attention over a period of time. One method for doing so is to link self-direction to work preparation. It is done by adding subheadings under "Work Preparation" to the rating form in Figure 6.1 that reflect self-direction. In programs designed to prepare unemployed and unskilled workers, the subheadings might relate to attendance, punctuality, meeting assignment deadlines, and setting learning goals—in continuing education programs, internships, and field placements. Additional subheadings might be used to reflect solving problems independently and taking responsibility for upgrading one's skills. In the spirit of promoting self-direction, it is important to involve the learners in establishing any and all instruments for assessing self-direction.

Portfolio assessment that involves learners in deciding what to include in the portfolio and what criteria to use in the assessment phase is well suited to self-directed learners. An educator can use portfolios with deeply dependent learners simply by specifying all that will go into the portfolio and exactly how it will be evaluated. The crucial point is that educators can promote self-direction by encouraging learners to assume more and more control of their portfolios and to assess their progress in assuming control. In this way the assessment procedure becomes a way of promoting development.

The comparison between the arithmetic and the teaching portfolios introduced at the beginning of this chapter can illustrate some of the aspects of assessing the portfolio as a whole. To be sure, each arithmetic paper would be assessed in terms of the number correct and performances might even be compared to the performance of other learners. But, the portfolio as a whole would be assessed in terms of broader considerations such as how well earlier material is transferred to more complex tasks later or how many arithmetic operations have been mastered. On the other hand, the teaching portfolio would be assessed in terms of the variety of the presentations, diversity in teaching skills, and suitability of assessments. In addition it would be assessed for consistency between philosophy and teaching performance. Finally, it would be assessed on the basis of evidence that the teacher had engaged in self-reflection and used feedback from peers and learners to plot a course for professional development. These assessments would not be based in any way on counting right answers but on ratings, preferably ratings based on scales anchored to specific criteria.

Ratings of individual performances and of the portfolio as a whole should be stored for future reference. Both the educator and the learner might keep copies, but at least one copy should be kept as part of the portfolio. The educator should record the name of the learner, the date the ratings were made, and the name and position of the person(s) who made the ratings. This information is crucial if portfolios are to be assessed repeatedly over a period of time—educators should assume they will be.

Rating instruments are used to promote valid assessments. They save time and effort because essential information is set down in standard form and does not need to be redone for each learner. As a result, they do not capture the style of individual learners so they usually need to be augmented with comments about the learners and their products which are stored along with the ratings. But even comments can be insufficient; portfolio conferences are typically needed to derive the full benefit from this approach to assessment.

Feedback Conferences

In many ways conferences between educator and learner are the most significant aspect of portfolio assessment. The conferences can take many forms, including telephone converstions and e-mail. Nonetheless, it seems that the most powerful is the face-to-face conference and that is the type that will be discussed here.

Conferences should be both frequent and long enough so that an educator and learner can thoroughly analyze the learner's situation, including the most recent learning products, the portfolio as a whole, and soon to be pursued learning goals. Both educator and learner should have ample opportunity to prepare for the conference by reviewing the portfolio in light of the rating instruments. They should each come to the conference with ideas about the strengths and weaknesses in the learner's performances, possible changes in learning behaviors, and future learning goals.

The educator should strive to be nondirective. Conferences should be more collaborative than didactic. The educator might begin by asking the learner to offer a statement of the strengths and weaknesses of the work. This request seems to (1) encourage self-assessment, (2) inform the learner that he or she is being treated respectfully, and (3) establish an alliance rather than an adversarial relationship with the learner. Next, the educator would respond to the points raised by the learner, taking care to avoid evaluation in the sense of judging the learner's performance as good or bad. The educator should control the conference only enough to have time to explain the ratings to the learner. The more references to detailed rubrics or benchmarks that can be woven into explanations, the easier it is to maintain objectivity during this section of the conference. Finally, the educator would point out progress whenever possible and act as a colleague in searching for ways to make subsequent learning activities effective for the learner.

In addition to conveying information and encouragement, the conferences provide a social aspect to the learning programs that approaches a coaching relationship (Moran 2001). The coaching can be especially helpful as learners acquire skills of self-evaluation. When a conference includes a question like, "What do you think are the best aspects of your work to date?" learners not only take a critical look at their work, but they anticipate similar questions in their upcoming conferences, and spend time reflecting on their work. With encouragement, they will soon be ready to address the question of what challenges they wish to take on next, which is a key to uncovering their talents and exercising their creativity.

Toward the end of the conference, the educator may have time to ask the learner for an assessment of the learning activities. The learners will appreciate the opportunity to switch roles. Not only do they sometimes provide helpful observations, but they inevitably begin to think of themselves as learners with distinct characteristics, some of which should be engendered and some modified. Overall, asking learners for their assessments, provides a good opportunity to end conferences on a pleasant note.

At the end of each conference, the educator should have a series of notes on the learner's progress that reflect the rating criteria. He or she should add a summary comment possibly describing special features that are unique about the individual learners. The only rule governing the notes and comments is that they should be encouraging even when the educator has no plans to share them with the learners. The rationale for the rule is that the tendency to encourage should pervade all an educator does, not to mention the possibility that learners might catch an unplanned glimpse of the notes.

Typically, the educator keeps the notes in his or her possession, but they are not intended to be a secret. They can be reviewed with the learner on the spot, copied for the learner, or incorporated into subsequent conferences. Learners might keep a parallel set of notes of their own making. In fact, such notes are a particularly good method for encouraging self-reflection which is an important goal subsumed under personal development.

Educator and learner conferences are the most important within portfolio assessment, but learner-learner conferences also have a significant role for at least three reasons. First, when an educator is working with a group of learners, peer assessment can be a time-saver. If two learners are examining one another's work while a third learner is conferencing with the educator, the two will be prepared to work efficiently when they meet with the educator. Second, receiving an assessment from a peer before presenting work to an educator may spur a learner to improve the work before showing it to the educator. Third, engaging in peer assessment is another way of learning assessment skills needed for self-assessment.

Ground rules are important for peer assessment to work. The educator probably would want to develop the rules with and for each group of learners. Generally, peers are expected to maintain strict confidentiality for all that transpires in the conferences, and to follow the same guidelines for giving feedback that educators observe.

Making Decisions

Portfolio assessment confronts an adult educator with issues of control rather directly. Looking back at the main logistical considerations, it seems clear that an educator could make all of the decisions or could turn over virtually all of the decisions to individual learners. Very often the decisions are made by the educator in consultation with the learners. For example, portfolios are sometimes used in technical areas such as computer assisted drafting where educators typically want to specify exactly what projects the learners attempt as a means of developing basic competencies in all the learners. They encourage learners who have developed the basic competencies to take on additional tasks of their own choosing. Of course, both the assigned and the chosen drafts become part of the portfolio. Often educators will want to collaborate with individual adult learners in making the decisions, and with each group work towards maximizing the control exercised by the learner as a way to promote self-direction.

EFFECTS OF LEARNER CONTROL

Since learners seem to have more influence on portfolio assessment than on any other form of educational assessment, it is important to analyze the nature of that influence. The following analysis is organized around the same four logistical issues mentioned above.

Choosing What Will Be Stored

Although there are no decisions about what will be stored in comprehensive portfolios, many such decisions are required for illustrative portfolios. First, there is the matter of criteria for inclusion. If learners decide to include only their best work, they will be accepting the responsibility for a considerable amount of self-assessment and as a result may develop a critical attitude towards their own work. If the portfolio is one that will be maintained over an extended period of time, they will be faced with the prospect of deleting items. This process can be difficult intellectually and even emotionally. Learners would probably have to make their decisions based on what they perceive as their learning goals and possibly their goals in life. All of these decisions engage learners in a level of introspection that is most appropriate for adults, but rarely achieved in other settings.

When learners decide which products should be stored, they opt for the products that most reflect their personalities as well as their learning interests. Involving learners in deciding what to include is likely to motivate them in their learning activities.

Choosing How Items Will Be Stored

Decisions about how material will be stored generally have their impact upon the practical aspects of portfolio management. Allowing learners to make decisions regarding storage is perhaps most helpful as a nonverbal message that they are being given responsibility for their learning. Unfortunately, a bad decision about how materials will be stored could be disastrous. Educators must be prepared to warn learners about possible pitfalls in their plans and even to override decisions if necessary. For example, if learners decide to store items on videotape when cameras or viewing facilities are limited, learners may become frustrated emotionally and may even be prevented from completing their tasks.

Rating Portfolios

There are several advantages to having input from learners in constructing rating instruments. These were set out in the previous chapter. Having learners actually make ratings is the issue here. Surely, they can offer formative assessment ratings—ratings that guide revisions but are not part of the final assessment—of their own work and their peers' work. And doing so is an excellent way to develop the habit of critical self-appraisal. Educators might even have learners take the primary responsibility for making formative assessments.

However, the situation is reversed for summative assessment. Learners will always form opinions of their completed work. And they should be encouraged to do so. But when summative assessments are recorded and transmitted as grades or references to potential employers or educational institutions, they should be based solely on the ratings of professional educators, not on the ratings of the learners or their peers.

Feedback Conferences

Clearly, conferences can be either teacher centered by emphasizing the educator's rating of the learners' performances, or learner centered by concentrating on the learners' self-evaluations and plans for future learning. The teacher-centered conferences are usually didactic. For example, if a learner had written limericks and haiku, a didactic approach would be to say, "Good. Now it is time to attempt a more demanding form. I want you to write a sonnet next." The learner-centered interactive approach in the same situation would be more like, "Good. Would you like to do something different? Have you thought about trying something like a sonnet?" Keeping in mind that there should be a general consistency from learning activities to assessment practices including conferences, educators might want to make the conferences as learner-centered and interactive as possible because the conferences seem to be among the most powerful means of promoting self-direction among learners.

GRADING PORTFOLIOS

Portfolio assessment is not particularly well suited for arriving at grades. To begin with, grading seems a violation of the collegial relationship that portfolio assessment tries to promote between educator and learner. In addition, the diversity in the learning goals that people pursue and in products of their learning makes it difficult to maintain a set of standards for rating different portfolios. Nonetheless, educators often do need to base grades on portfolio assessments, and their best guides are the methods that were described for performance assessments.

Analytical scoring would be done by averaging grades for each item in the portfolio. Holistic scoring would probably require a rating instrument developed for the purpose. Learning progress, versatility, creativity, and self-direction would be among the aspects rated.

THE SELF-DIRECTED PORTFOLIO

Thus far the descriptions have been of portfolios that are developed within structured learning programs involving an educator and at least a small group of learners. However, portfolios can be self-directed and many professionals are choosing to direct portfolios to promote their own professional development. Educators at all levels from nursery school to graduate school and adult and continuing education have become enthusiastic about what are usually called teaching portfolios (Murray, 1995). The primary reason for maintaining a teaching portfolio is to improve one's teaching by analyzing materials in order to identify strengths, weaknesses, and avenues for growth. Increasingly, educators submit teaching portfolios as evidence of their qualifications when the apply for positions and promotions.

Teaching Portfolios

The teaching portfolio that was mentioned at the beginning of this chapter is given additional detail at this point in order to explicate the characteristics of self-directed portfolios and to serve as an example for adult educators who might have an interest in directing a teaching portfolio of their own.

Documented Preparation for Teaching

This section is more like something found in a resume than are the other sections. It emphasizes the educator's background in teaching and in subject matter. It would likely include a list of educational degrees, prior positions relevant to teaching, and recommendations from supervisors.

Description of Teaching Responsibilities

This section explains exactly what content areas the educator covers and the types of learners involved. It describes the predominate learning goals as they are set by the educator, the learners, and/or stakeholders.

Statement of Philosophy of Teaching

The statement of philosophy serves to explain what is distinctive about the educator rather than to state truisms such as a pledge to help all people become all they can be. For example, it might include a statement of preferred teaching/learning methods.

Sample Lesson Plans and Teaching Materials

The plans can be simple descriptions, but the materials should be presented just as they are presented to the learners. For example, overhead transparencies could be packaged with the text. Physical objects used in demonstrations might have to be photographed. The samples should be arranged to illustrate how the educator implements his or her philosophy of teaching and how the learning activities match the learning goals.

Sample Assessment Systems and Materials

Assessment systems should be related to learning goals. Paper and pencil tests could be reproduced and included just as they were given to the learners. Sample portfolios produced by learners could also be included. Methods of interpretation, including grading systems when used, would be explained. It is important to explain explicitly how the philosophy of teaching is implemented in the assessment procedures.

Videotaped Demonstrations of Teaching

Videotaped demonstrations are unmatched as a way of characterizing teaching/presentation skills. They are a bit threatening so simply including them represents a firm commitment to improving one's practice.

Learners' Products

Anything that learners produce could be included, and it is important to display some of their work. It is also problematic because it is normally hard to include a large enough number to avoid the suspicion that only the few most impressive learner products were included. Portfolios can be especially helpful in resolving the problem because they are relatively compact collections of work produced over time so they can be examined for evidence of learner progress which is a valid reflection of the educator's effectiveness.

Assessments of Teaching from Supervisors, Peers, and Learners

Organization is the most important issue here. One approach is to arrange the assessments chronologically first for supervisors, then for peers, and finally for learners. This facilitates making assessments of progress, especially of how well the educator has responded to earlier criticisms.

Statement of Professional Development History, Goals, and Activities

As much as anything this is where educators display their capacity for self-reflection and growth. There should be detailed accounts of what efforts were made to improve their practices in response to assessments made by themselves and others. Examples of such efforts would be modifications in plans and/or materials and consultations with staff development experts. Similarly there should be explanations of how educators stay current in their content area. Professional reading, conference attendance, credit-bearing courses are evidence of those efforts.

Criteria and Rating Scales for Judging Performance

An educator might wish to develop a highly specific rubric for assessing the evidence in a teaching portfolio. But a less specific rating scale might do as well or better because it makes it easier for peers or supervisors to use it during conferences with the educator. An example of a less specific scale is found in Figure 6.2. It has been constructed so that it could be used by the owner of the portfolio and by a peer or supervisor who is not familiar with the educator's field.

Sometimes a teaching portfolio can be strengthened by adding comments to highlight how the sections of the portfolio relate to each other. For example, some educators place a page at the beginning of the sections on lesson plans and assessment systems to explain how the materials in these sections reflect their teaching philosophies as well as what is distinctive about their teaching. Educators should feel free to add similar comments to any or all sections.

The one statement that will always be true about teaching portfolios is that they are all different. Nonetheless, there are some features that seem essential. Since portfolios are developed over a number of years, they should be illustrative rather than

For each criteria summarize the evidence presented in the portfolio and then assign a rating from 1 to 5 using the following key:

1 clearly below professional level

2 some questionable practice indicated

3 professional practice throughout

4 some evidence of superior practice

5 considerable evidence of superior practice

Evidence that teaching preparation suits teaching responsibilities

Rating _____

Evidence that professional philosophy is implemented in practice

Rating _____

Evidence of versatility in teaching/learning and assessment methods

Rating _____

Evidence of creativity in design of learning materials, activities, and assessment methods

Rating _____

Evidence of teaching/presentation skills

Rating _____

Evidence of teaching effectiveness

Rating _____

Evidence of professional development

Rating _____

Figure 6.2 Rating Scale for Assessing a Teaching Portfolio

comprehensive. As a result, materials are always being added and deleted. Although they might document the development of an educator's skills, they should emphasize his or her current practice. The materials offered as evidence of skill should also showcase the educator's vision, versatility, and commitment to teaching. Throughout the portfolio, there should be an emphasis on evidence of self-assessment and consequent efforts to improve.

EVEN IF YOU DON'T USE PORTFOLIOS

At the end of this chapter on portfolio assessment, it is important to recognize that there will be many educators who decide not to use portfolios. They may find that portfolios require too much effort, take away too much time from learning activities, or are less suited to their subject matter than other methods. However, it seems that the current emphasis on portfolios does have two important reminders even for adult educators who do not use them. Primary is the value of personal communication that is facilitated in the conferences. The conference format allows educators and learners to collaborate in assessing what has been accomplished and in planning what will be undertaken next. It also enables educators to advise and encourage as much as to assess. Since conferences can be held around a single piece of work and as part of any learning program, they are available to educators regardless of whether they use portfolios. The second point is a reminder to all educators to make assessments as lifelike as possible.

ASSESSMENT IN SPECIFIC SITUATIONS

Having reviewed the major principles and procedures of informal assessment, it is time to examine how they are applied in specific situations. The next chapter is devoted to applications in settings such as community education, General Equivalency Diploma (GED) programs, and higher education.

CHAPTER 7

Applying Assessment Strategies

Assessment always seems to require adapting principles and strategies to fit the nuances of specific situations. In this chapter, some of the likely adaptations for a few adult education settings are mentioned. They are intended to be examples of how the material in the earlier chapters might be applied and modified, and definitely are not a comprehensive account of what educators have done or should do in these settings. This chapter is written with the view that each learning program must capitalize on some forms of assessment and exclude others in order to preserve time and resources to achieve its learning objectives. Even though all adult education settings are unique, it is hoped that readers will find something to apply to their home settings in each of the examples.

ADULT BASIC EDUCATION

Learners in Adult Basic Education (ABE) settings are like learners in all other settings in being marvelously diverse. Some may have a high school diploma and be working to upgrade skills while others may never reach GED level. They differ in aptitude for learning, attitude toward learning, learning styles, and objectives for learning. Therefore, their educators need a broad spectrum of assessment skills.

As a group, ABE learners do not have particularly positive educational histories. Therefore, one of the challenges in serving them is to monitor their progress without threatening their self-esteem. It seems that the threat comes not so much from the assessment per se as it does from a sense that assessment leads to grading and the possibility of failing.

Therefore, adult educators are well advised to decouple assessment from grading in as many ways as possible. A no-nonsense explanation of the importance of ungraded formative evaluation is a good idea. But nonverbal messages are among the most powerful, so placing formative assessment in a game format seems a particularly good idea. The atmosphere created by games counteracts a learner's tendency to catastrophize, and makes it likely that he or she will be able to recognize the help that assessment activities are in promoting learning by identifying what has been learned, and what has to be reviewed before moving on to new material. Sternberger (1995) has presented some excellent ideas for adapting crossword puzzles, bingo, and Jeopardy to ABE classrooms in order to conduct formative assessment and facilitate learning.

Summative assessment need not be terribly different. As long as grades are not given, assessment can be conducted without marked threat. The basic principle is to provide information regarding relative strengths and weaknesses, domains mastered, or still to be mastered, while avoiding comparisons among learners or pass/fail types of pronouncements.

GED

From a national perspective, GED classes are a large and important part of adult education. They provide an opportunity for many adults to improve their lives by upgrading their educational attainments. They also provide a service to the country by greatly increasing the literacy, numeracy, and critical thinking of the citizenry. One of the distinguishing characteristics of GED learning is that it is designed to prepare individuals to pass an examination which is developed by neither the GED learners nor their educators.

Having a national GED examination with definite cutoff

scores for passing, gives the diploma immediate credibility. After all, it is the same assessment system that is used for many professional licenses. On the other hand, having a national examination exerts considerable top-down control that may put learners in a passive or dependent mode. The learners must work toward the exam in a number of ways. First, they must study the material that is on the test and so relinquish their voice in determining what to learn. Second, they need to constantly monitor their progress with formative assessments that are modeled after the GED examination and so relinquish their voice in how they will be assessed.

As tools for this type of formative assessment informal paper and pencil tests have considerable utility. Skillful educators can construct as many tests as are needed to identify specific learning needs of individual learners. For example, if a group of learners were working on fractions in mathematics, items can be generated to determine what, if any, difficulties individual learners were having with various aspects of fractions. The educator could write a cluster of computation problems to identify who was struggling with and needing help with converting to least common denominator or dividing fractions by fractions.

These informal tests can use the same types of items as the GED examination, but they are relatively low on the scale of intimidating instruments. They can be made even less threatening, possibly encouraging, by training learners to interpret the results of the tests. Learners who can participate in identifying their strengths and weaknesses as well as planning remedial learning and choosing future learning activities will become more effective learners.

Interactive communication skills are particularly important for educators who are involving learners in these types of interpretations. They are pretty much the same skills that are needed in other educational settings, such as portfolio conferences. In particular, educators would probably strive to collaborate in making interpretations in order to both mentor the learner in self-assessment and to be sure the learner was properly directed in preparing for the GED examination.

WORKPLACE

Perhaps the distinguishing characteristic of workplace education is that its purpose is primarily to further the goals of the employer. Nonetheless, employers (or supervisors), trainees, and educators might collaborate in the entire educational planning process from stating objectives to formatting the learning activities and developing the assessment instruments as a way of achieving efficient training with successful transfer of learning to job performance. They often find that expectancy grids are helpful in setting achievement standards and evaluating learning activities.

Consider a business that must have workers who perform several intricate procedures in order to work in a dust-free environment. Initially, trainers would collaborate with supervisors and experienced workers to plan the learning and assessment activities. Next, they would chart the performance of trainees on summative assessments against performance on the job the first week after training. The chart would reveal what level of performance on the summative assessments were associated with job success.

Figure 7.1 illustrates the use of an expectancy grid. In this simplified case, the number of errors on the job is related to the summative training assessment rating. It seems clear that all learners should achieve a rating of at least 4 before they leave the training. The chart also reveals that 30 out of the 50 trainees did not reach the criterion of 4 on the performance assessment. With 60% of trainees failing to achieve mastery, it is clear that the training about dressing procedures needs to be improved.

COMMUNITY EDUCATION

Although adults often attend community education to pursue learning objectives that are job related, community education differs from workplace education in being far more learner centered. Very often learners decide that they want to acquire skills that they cannot get within the parameters of their jobs.

	Number of dressing errors reported by supervisors during first 5 days of work following training					
	0	1	2	3	4	5 or more
Performance rating by trainer for dust-free dressing						
1					1	6
2					4	6
3		1	4	5		
4	5	5				
5	5	5				

Figure 7.1 Expectancy Grid Presenting the Relationship of Performance of 50 Workers during Training and on the Job

In addition, they want those newly acquired skills certified in some fashion. Actual certificates are issued in a number of ways. When community agencies award certificates in areas such as computer skills and secretarial skills, they are often based on attendance. This is the case for American Management Association courses. Graduates of these courses sometimes decide to support the certificates with portfolios that display their accomplishments. A second type of certificate is exemplified by the Red Cross certificate for lifesaving which is awarded for passing a criterion-referenced examination with paper and pencil and performance sections administered by registered examiners. On the other hand, when certificates are approved by a college or university, evaluation is very similar to that of undergraduate courses—norm-referenced paper and pencil tests.

Of course, many times learners in community education centers are not looking for certified qualifications. Other examples are the learners pursuing personal development goals. They might want to become more informed investors, more competent quilters, more knowledgeable churchgoers, more effective parents, or more self-accepting. In all of these cases, assessment needs a different orientation, an orientation based on holistic self-assessment.

Holistic Assessment

Holistic assessment (not to be confused with holistic rating) is particularly useful in community education because it helps learners examine their learning from several perspectives. The basic idea is to have learners respond to general questions about their learning. The actual questions presented to learners vary with the situation although the system seems to work best when they are open-ended and require a written response. Figure 7.2 contains examples of questions that might be asked of sophisticated learners in a community education program that had an academic and personal development orientation. The rationale for these questions appears below.

What did you learn about the topics in this course of study?

Name, date, and description of course of study are for possible record keeping and could be omitted. However, a question about the stated objectives of the learning program is almost always needed. It assumes that all the learners are clear about the objectives which may have been listed in a course description, but preferably, had been developed with the learners at the outset of the learning program. The question is not designed to elicit a detailed list of knowledge level material. Instead it is intended to get learners to look back at their efforts and indicate what was most significant to them.

What did you learn about topics related to this course of study?

As an example of learning about topics related to the stated learning objectives, consider a person who is taking a course on parenting and goes to the library for a book on that topic. In scanning the shelves he or she might become intrigued by a title

---

The purpose of this exercise is to help you reflect on your learning experience. Please comment on each of the following. Write as much or as little as you wish; just respond in whatever way seems best to you.

Name _____   Date _____

Describe the course of study your comments will be referring to.

What did you learn about the topics in this course of study?

What did you learn about topics related to this course of study?

How has your view of learning and knowledge changed?

How has your view of yourself changed?

What plans are you making for future learning activities?

What additional comments seem significant to you?

Figure 7.2 Sample Holistic Assessment Form

and read a book on caring for aging parents. Asking about such learning may result in some blank stares and empty stretches on the response sheet, but it always serves the purpose of reminding learners to reach out and explore the intellectual world independently.

How has your view of learning and knowledge changed?

A question about the nature of learning and knowledge is a challenge to almost everyone so educators may need to explain some of the ways it might be answered. One possibility is to answer in terms of learning styles. Of course, that is more of a possibility if the concept of learning style has been discussed during the learning program. A second approach is to answer in terms of cognitive development. Several theorists (Moran, 1991) have described stages in the development of an adult understanding of the nature and/or limitations of human knowledge. It is a considerable oversimplification, but one necessary for the flow of this chapter, to say that the theorists believe that preadult learners typically hold the view that statements of knowledge on a given point are immutably either right or wrong. As a result they strive to memorize what they are told is correct information. They seem to be like the dependent learners in Grow's model (see Chapter 1). According to the theorists, these learners must go through a process of several years to achieve an understanding of knowledge as relative within systems of thought, generated from evidence by people, and subject to change. Adult educators have been encouraged to spend a great deal of time and effort trying to create learning situations that help learners reach the more advanced levels of understanding of (Moran, 1991). Asking learners to explain how their views of knowledge have changed gives them the opportunity to consolidate their insights into the nature of knowledge and experience a sense of progress as reflected in comments like, "I learned that there really aren't any right or wrong answers in this area." Educators who hear these comments should take the opportunity to reinforce that development.

How has your view of yourself changed?

Adult education is often transformational (Mezirow, 1991). Asking learners how they have transformed themselves gives support to those who have done so. For those who have not engaged in introspection the question is an invitation to do so in the future. Since so many community education programs emphasize personal development, it is noted that when development is discussed in a learning program, learners could be asked to use the language and concepts from those discussions to describe themselves. For example, in a course on investing, learners might explain why they have become more conservative or aggressive; in a course for returning adult learners, they might describe themselves in terms of Grow's model for development from dependent to self-directed learners.

What plans are you making for future learning activities?

This question highlights the continuous nature of adult education, and coming at the end of the form, it encourages learners to plan in terms of both specific learning goals and broad personal or professional goals. In fact, this question is as much an attempt to get learners to make plans for learning as it is a question about the plans they may have made.

What additional comments seem significant to you?

Asking for additional comments is highly recommended. Adult learners are simply too diverse and creative for an educator to be able to anticipate all they have to say. Not only will their comments be helpful, but the learners will appreciate the mark of respect that comes from being asked.

Conducting Holistic Assessment

The holistic assessment can be adapted for use in most adult education programs. Not only can the specific questions be selected for the situation, but the information collection and interpretation can be conducted in many ways. Of course, holistic assessment should not be a surprise that the educator springs on the learners at the end of learning program; it should be introduced to them early in the program and revisited several times during the program. Some educators might prefer to distribute a form similar to Figure 7.2 at the outset of a program so that learners who are unfamiliar with the process have ample time to prepare for it. Others might wait for a sense of community to develop within the learners and then involve them in developing their own set of questions. In either case, it is a good idea to remind learners of the process at several points during the learning program.

Another major issue is whether learners will keep their assessments private or share them in some formal fashion. Assessments that are kept private are beneficial for the learners and take no time away from learning. However, sharing can be so meaningful that it is most often the better decision. Two methods for sharing the holistic assessments are described below.

Conferences

Holistic assessment conferences are perhaps best conducted as portfolio assessment conferences are conducted. In fact, holistic and portfolio assessment have so much in common that many educators will want to incorporate holistic assessment questions into their portfolio systems. The conferences are nondirective. The learners are encouraged to say what they want about themselves while the facilitator listens carefully, seeks clarification occasionally, and encourages persistently. Although it is true that the educator can learn a great deal about what is meaningful to learners in these conferences, the emphasis should be on listening to the learner as a person and reflecting how much the learners have gotten from the learning program and their self-assessment.

It is recommended that the conferences follow the sequence of the holistic assessment questions. This practice gives the learners the opportunity to recognize their achievements at the outset of the conference and often results in a time of quiet celebration. However, some learners become surprisingly self-critical in these conferences. Educators do not need to agree or disagree with the self-criticisms. It is better to listen and offer support whenever the conversation turns toward the future and what the learner might want to do differently.

As the conferences progress, educators must be careful to avoid questioning the learners because questions are a way of controlling interactions. Learners who ask questions should get meaningful answers, but the educator should remain nondirective. Those asking for advice might be given alternatives to choose from or sources of information. It seems preferable to be encouraging rather than authoritative. Educators should be very clear in expressing appreciation to any learners who share holistic assessments with them.

Groups

Sharing groups are important alternatives to individual conferences for holistic assessment. This approach seems particularly appropriate when group cohesion is known or expected to be high as is normally the case in learning activities devoted to personal and/or professional development. It is also a good choice when the learners are talented people who have the capacity to teach and learn from one another.

The group sharing approach does require planning and preparation. Educators would want to describe the process and have a clear indication that the learners wish to participate. The learners should take part in developing the list of assessment questions. They should have many group activities during their learning program so that they are skilled at group processes. The educator would explain that the purpose of the group session is for each individual to assess his or her own learning and for each individual to learn from one another. Therefore, no one should assess another person in the group or divulge any comments made during the session to those outside of the group.

One good way to open is to explain that each person will have the opportunity to share his or her response on each of the assessment questions, but that no one is expected to comment on all of the assessment questions. The educator might lead by offering his or her personal response to the first question and then invite learners to give theirs. After each person has responded or passed on the first question, the educator or volunteers would summarize the comments of the group. This procedure would continue until all the assessment questions have been covered and the total process characterized by the group.

Educators are wise to take notes on the summary statements. They will contain information about what is significant to learners, what personal development they achieved, what they wish to learn about and how to improve the learning for similar groups yet to be served.

In situations where the group is large or the list of assessment questions so long that the process would be cumbersome, any number of adaptations are suitable. It would be no problem to divide the sharing process over more than one meeting or to break into small groups of five to seven. Any organization of the sharing is appropriate as long as it allows everyone to be heard by an attentive group.

It should be added that holistic assessment is closely associated with the work of Long (1990) who has amply demonstrated that it is certainly not limited to community education applications. It is particularly helpful for self-directed learning and in higher education.

HIGHER EDUCATION

Higher education is the term used to describe regionally accredited postsecondary institutions that offer academic degrees. The degrees vary from the two-year Associate of Arts degrees to graduate Ph.D's, JD's, and MD's. Sometimes higher education institutions award certificates testifying to the completion of other programs, but the degree programs are the distinguishing features of institutions of higher education.

Within higher education, assessment has long been a matter of paper and pencil tests with some areas, such as student teaching, using performance assessments and others, such as visual arts, using portfolios. The system, though not perfect, has been workable because it matches with the traditional learning methods of reading textbooks and taking notes on lectures, and because it leads to individual grades for individual learners which can be recorded in the registrar's office as a permanent evaluation of achievement.

Recently cooperative education has been proposed as more effective than the traditional learning methods. Trice (2000) asserted that "[c]ollaborative work is the most vital topic in education, from nursery school through graduate school" (p. 291). He went on to state that the impetus for the interest in collaborative work or group work as it is often called comes from two sources. Industry has called for workers who are skilled in working in teams, and feminist scholars have called for educational practices that are less hierarchical and more cooperative. Many adult educators inside and outside of higher education have responded to these calls by incorporating group activities into their instructional plans.

Johnson, Johnson, and Smith (1998) made a strong case for the effectiveness of cooperative group learning as an instructional method on the basis of an extensive review of research. They concluded that cooperative learning activities are very effective in achieving a variety of goals, and particularly effective for improving problem-solving skills. Readers can find an excellent summary of cooperative learning procedures in Johnson, Johnson, and Smith (1998). Generally, in cooperative learning, a group is assigned a task and in turn the group assigns responsibilities to its individual members. If everyone fulfills his or her responsibility, the group accomplishes the task, which is likely to be writing a report or making a class presentation, and everybody in the group learns a great deal about the topic and about working with others. It is important for educators to provide learners with instruction, practice, and feedback regarding their performance in cooperative work prior to making assignments on which students are graded on their group work. In fact it is a violation of good practice for an educator to grade learners on anything except what that educator has helped the learners accomplish.

Not surprisingly, assessing the learning that takes place as the result of group work is a complex matter. First, individual learners often perform tasks that are so varied that educators cannot accurately compare the relative effort and achievement of the learners within a group. Second, even if it were possible to assess learners solely on the basis of their individual contributions, that procedure probably would defeat the purposes of the group assignment. It would minimize the stake that individuals have in the success of the group to the point of transforming the learning activity into a set of independent projects. Third, assigning all the members of a group the same grade can create difficulties. Assessments based solely on group products provide an opportunity for some learners to rely on the more conscientious members of the group to do their work for them. When this happens, the more conscientious members of the group feel exploited; the less conscientious members fail to achieve the learning objectives; and no one learns the right lessons about working in teams. Some critics have charged that group grading could allow some learners to graduate from degree programs primarily on the achievements of others, and that the only advantage of cooperative learning is that educators never have the discomfort of telling learners they are not doing well. Fourth, assessments of group work are problematic as a basis for assessing learning programs because there is always the possibility that one member of a group might have produced a satisfactory or excellent final product misleading the educator into concluding that all members of the group learned well.

Combination strategies (Johnson, Johnson, and Smith, 1998; Trice, 2000) that assess learners on their individual work, on a single product produced by the group, and on their contributions to the group process seem best. The prototypical combination strategy is to assign a project in which all the group members conduct a comparable portion of the project individually and then collaborate on a synthesis of their individual work. For example, in a program to prepare adults to enter the workforce, each of four learners could locate, read, and report on an article on how to interview for a job. The learners would be encouraged to help one another in ways such as sharing information, but each learner would have ultimate responsibility for his or her report. As a group they would submit one document composed of the individual reports sandwiched between an introduction written collaboratively and a summary written collaboratively. Each learner would receive an individual grade for the quality of his or her report, the same grade as everyone else in the group for the quality of the introduction and summary, and an individual grade for his or her contributions to the collaborative process.

As indicated in Chapter 5, educators bear the responsibility for grading the learners. Therefore, they proceed by assigning grades for the individual work and collaborative work by using rubrics just as they normally grade assignments. However, they often need to take a different approach in assessing the contributions of individuals to the group process. They can assign scores for contributions to the group if and only if they have had sufficient opportunities to observe the individuals participate in the group activities. If they do not have ample opportunities to observe the group activities, and this is commonly the case, they can have the learners use the rubrics to assign scores to one another. The educators then can convert the scores derived from the rubrics into grades.

Usually all the members of a group use the same rubric to assign a score between 1 and 100 to every member of the group including themselves. Having group members assign scores to one another runs two substantial risks. First, it tempts learners to assign low scores to the members of their groups in order to obtain a relatively higher grade for themselves (Simpson, 1995). When learners adopt this strategy, they vitiate the assessment process and they undermine the efforts of the educator to encourage cooperation and related group skills. Second, it tempts learners to collude in assigning every member of the group the same high score for contributing to group work in order to ensure they all receive a high grade. When learners adopt this strategy, they clearly subvert the assessment process. It may be argued that they are learning to cooperate with one another; however, this argument is short sighted because it fails to recognize that the learners have failed to cooperate with the educator and all others who have an interest in the assessment.

One way to minimize these risks is to require learners to justify the number of points they assign to the members of their groups. It seems that learners rarely yield to the temptations described above when they examine the facts of each person's participation. It must be said that this procedure is more effective when educators train the learners in how to assign points and give justifications. In particular they should be instructed to add descriptions of the specific comments and actions of the group members on which they based the assignment of points. Some examples of justifications for high ratings follow: Alpha took notes on the group discussion and wrote the first draft of the summary. Beta resolved a conflict that developed between two other group members. Some examples of justifications for low ratings follow: Delta never said anything during our meetings. Epsilon agreed with everything everybody said, but never contributed an original idea.

Having learners justify the scores they assign seems to improve the validity of the scores, and provides three additional benefits. First, it enhances the self-assessment each learner conducts. Second, it provides material for educators to use when they give feedback to learners regarding their group skills. Third, it provides material for educators to use when they write reference letters.

A very different way to proceed is to have each member of the group apportion a fixed number of points (usually 100 points) among the members of the group for their contributions to the group effort. There are two clear advantages to this system. First, with a limit of 100 for all the members of the group, the system eliminates the possibility that the learners might subvert the assessment by rating everyone either high or low. Second, learners quickly see that if there are 100 points to be divided among five group members, for one member to receive more than 20 points someone else must receive fewer than 20 points. This competitive aspect of the system motivates learners to contribute to the project. Unfortunately, the competition among group members often turns their interactions into contests for points rather than exercises in cooperation.

Some educators reject the fixed-number of points system as being overly competitive. Others adopt it on the grounds that in the world of work competition and cooperation are always intertwined and that this system is beneficial precisely because it is an authentic example of what learners must deal with in the workplace.

Educators who adopt the fixed-number of points method should require learners to justify the number of points they assign to group members. However, they should think twice before deciding whether or not they have the learners apportion points to themselves as well as to the other members of the group. On the one hand, having learners apportion points to themselves involves them in potentially valuable self-assessment. On the other hand, it may heighten the competitive aspects of the assessment to where the assessment becomes distorted. For example, some learners may rate themselves overly high in the interests of getting a favorable rating while others strive to be fair to all and still others rate themselves too low out of a sense of guilt. Given that the system is inherently competitive, it may be wise to minimize the competition by having learners rate only the other members of the group and not themselves. Educators who use the fixed-point method and wish to have learners conduct self-assessments of their behavior in groups can incorporate such self-assessments in other activities. For example, they can make them part of the holistic assessments described earlier in this chapter.

It is not clear that the fixed-number of points system is superior to a system in which every group member can be assigned any score from the highest to the lowest possible score. Educators may need to experiment with the two approaches to see which works better with their learners. It is clear that in both systems educators need to convince learners to evaluate one another conscientiously, to provide learners with usable rubrics, and to require learners to state their reasons for the points they assign to group members.

Finally, although there are good reasons to have learners assess the contributions of group members to the group activities, there are also times when learners will resist. Sometimes the resistance is stated as an inability to distinguish the value of one good idea versus a number of lesser contributions. Sometimes it is stated as sense that assessment violates the relationships that build up in a group. Whenever learners express resistance, educators are well advised to discuss the matter thoroughly with the learners. They should give a full explanation for the assignment and for the assessment procedures, taking care to attend to the feelings of the learners. If the learners are unconvinced, the educator probably should collaborate with them to revise the peer assessment procedures. Refusing to revise the system is quite likely to lower morale and compromise the entire learning program. However, after they revise the assessment procedure, educators should search for ways to bring those learners to the point where they have the inclination and the skills to engage in meaningful evaluation of their peers at least in the area of contributions to group work.

Clearly cooperative learning can and should be used in adult education settings outside higher education. Cooperative learning and particularly the issues associated with assessing learning that takes place in cooperative groups were considered in this section on higher education only because those issues are most complicated in higher education where greater emphasis is put on grading. Fortunately, the combination strategy developed to address the complications arising from the demands for grading are equally effective in settings where no grades are given. Learners can examine their individual learning in the light of standards, perhaps stated in rubrics, and compare what they have produced to what others have produced. Learners can also give and receive feedback about their role in the group process. Similarly, educators can assess the effectiveness of their programs on the same dimensions.

It is important to close this section by noting that to this point the discussion has centered on norm-referenced assessment where widely shared objective standards of achievement do not exist and learners commonly experience a sense of competition. Almost everything seems to change when learners are facing criterion-referenced tasks on which they will receive individual scores and grades. Regardless of whether the scores and grades are assigned by their teacher/educator or by some outside agent, criterion-referenced tasks can be managed to create a sense of cooperation rather than competition. The very fact of the impending assessment creates the potential for group cohesion. Educators can encourage further cooperation by asking learners to share resources, meet in study groups, tutor one another, and discuss the benefits of cooperative learning. A good example is a group of non-native speakers of English preparing to take a test of English language proficiency. Whether they are in higher education, community education, or other programs, they will inform, motivate, and support one another in ways that educators alone often cannot.

SELF-DIRECTED LEARNING

If cooperative learning is currently one of the most vital topics in all of education, self-directed learning remains one of the more attractive concepts in adult education. It empowers learners in calling them to decide what they will learn, how they will learn, and how they will assess what they have learned. As Grow (1991) has implied, people are not dependent or self-directed learners by nature. Certain people develop from dependence to self-direction over a considerable period of time depending in large part on their educational experiences. Part of that developmental process consists of acquiring skills in selecting learning goals, conducting learning activities, and assessing learning.

Some learners seem to acquire those skills incidentally by observing the assessment practices of their educators. Nonetheless, educators can promote self-direction by providing direct instruction in these skills. Educators can provide instruction in assessment in at least five ways. First, they can demonstrate to learners the process by which they plan assessments. For example, they could display and analyze their planning grids with their learners (See Chapter 3). In doing so they would explain to learners the levels of knowing from knowledge through synthesis and evaluation. They would also explain the process of selecting learning products that reflect achievement of different levels of knowing. Second, educators could involve learners in planning assessments. For example, they could collaborate with learners in preparing planning grids and in developing assessment instruments such as rating scales and rubrics. Third, educators could involve learners in peer assessments and self-assessments. Fourth, educators can assign learning contracts and spend conference time helping learners develop and refine their assessment plans. Fifth, they can connect learners with resources such as books, articles, and experts on informal educational assessment. Each of these strategies for imparting assessment skills can increase the likelihood that adults will become successful self-directed learners.

Finally, the term self-directed learning has acquired the connotation of independent individual work; however, self-directed learning can also be collaborative learning. When two or more learners share a self-directed project, they can use the combination strategy described in the previous section to assess their individual learning as well their group work and what they learned about how to work collaboratively. Educators can help by explaining the strategy to them, and participating in their efforts to adapt the strategy to their specific projects.

CONTINUING PROFESSIONAL EDUCATION

In continuing professional education, there is every reason to operate on the assumption that the learners are motivated to use informal assessment information to improve their expertise. When psychologists attend a workshop to learn to use a personality test, they want to administer the test, score it, and interpret it. Administering and scoring are usually straightforward tasks that they practice on their own, and then they want to be observed and approved by an expert. Interpretation is not so straightforward. It entails judgment, and they want to compare their interpretations with those of several colleagues. The opportunity to make those comparisons in roundtable activities is often the assessment procedure they prefer.

There is a similar approach that can be carried out on a distance basis as well as on a classroom/workshop basis. It consists of administering an objective test and presenting the professionals with detailed feedback on how well they did. The feedback would include the items they had right and wrong as well as what percentage of their colleagues had those items correct. Assuming that the test has been made to reflect the knowledge base of the profession, this statistical type of feedback gives the test takers the information they need in order to decide what topics they wish to study in order to maintain or improve their professional knowledge. This type of assessment is a clear example of the principle that the purpose of assessment is to improve learning.

LOOKING AHEAD

At this point, the established principles of informal assessment have been described. There is one major set of considerations that needs to addressed. It is the emerging issues in assessment. They are addressed in the final chapter.

CHAPTER 8

Current and Continuing Issues

In Chapter 7 we looked at how assessment addresses different concerns in different settings. In this final chapter, we consider how the principles of informal assessment pertain to four issues that arise in virtually every adult education setting. They are (1) achieving coherence among assessment activities within an educational agency, (2) dealing with multiculturalism and diversity, (3) promoting professional development among educators, and (4) maintaining ethical practices.

COHERENCE AMONG ASSESSMENT ACTIVITIES

One of the enduring issues in the profession of education is the conflict between the preference of individual educators to carry out their professional duties free of constraints and the desire of those who have a stake in the quality of education for assurances that educators develop and observe established practices. The conduct of informal assessment is a case in point.

In Chapter 1 informal assessment was described as a set of established principles that work best when they are applied by educators exercising their professional judgment. In practice, the concept of academic freedom, which was developed in higher education at the beginning of this century, apparently contributed to a tendency among all educators to follow their inclinations more than the principles described by experts in deciding how to assess learning. However, when educators within an institution use radically different assessment activities, there is a risk that those techniques will be perceived as an incoherent jumble that is arbitrary, unwelcome, and possibly unfair with the result that assessment becomes a point of contention between learners and educators.

To minimize this risk, the educators within an institution do well to develop policies regarding the assessment practices that are appropriate for the institution as well as guidelines and illustrations of their use. Examples of the kinds of guidelines that educators might choose are presented below.

The religious education staff within an institution might choose to avoid tests of learner achievement but use other techniques for assessing the learning process. They might agree to each conduct at least one assessment of the learning process in their learning programs. Appropriate activities might include the Critical Incident technique and the All Thumbs procedure mentioned in Chapter 2. Within a short period, the learners would become adept at responding to these opportunities, and the staff members could share their findings for the purpose of improving their assessments of learning activities.

Educators in situations where grades are assigned may want to coordinate their assessment activities for assessing learning achievement. For example, they might recommend that a minimum number of graded activities be employed in each course, that there be variety in the modes of assessment, that all courses have a final examination, and that all final examinations be filed in a department office.

It might take considerable time and effort for a group of educators to reach consensus. For example, educators who use portfolio assessments would not be satisfied with guidelines for filing final exams. They may want to have space allocated for storing copies of portfolios of graduates instead. Fortunately, any discussion of assessment is likely to provoke reflection and improve practice.

Learner input is a feature that most institutions would want to address in their assessment policies. In keeping with the position that adult learners should be involved in the assessment of their own learning, each agency should have a procedure for analyzing the thoughts of learners regarding the assessment practices of the institution. It might be accomplished with a survey distributed to a sample of learners at the institution.

Finally, it is recommended that each institution have a standing committee that reviews and updates the institutional policy on a yearly basis. The committee might take on some issues that have political as well as educational dimensions. Two that come to mind are grading standards and dealing with learners who appear to be cheating. Both of these issues are considered below, but for the moment, it is noted that individual educators can benefit from the guidance and support of institution sponsored committees when practice touches political concerns.

Grading Standards

Grading was discussed from the standpoint of the individual educator in Chapter 4. One of the points was that a learner's grade should be more a function of achievement than of the grading practices of the educator. Toward that end, it was recommended that each educator curve letter grades to a distribution chosen by the institution. Individual educators would always have the option of departing from the distribution, but they would use the distribution to orient to the norm for the institution.

Here the discussion turns to deciding what the distribution of letter grades should be—what percentage of grades should be As, Bs, and so on. The decision presents a dilemma: Institutions fear giving such low grades that their graduates will be penalized in comparison to graduates from schools with more lenient standards. They also want to be rigorous in demanding excellence in exchange for an A. One way to address the dilemma is to confer with comparable neighboring institutions and pursue a consensus on a distribution of grades. In this way no institution need be out of step.

Another procedure is to make grades more interpretable for

learners, employers, and other educational institutions by presenting the information about the actual grading standards by including class rank whenever grade point averages are provided. If one school reported that a person had a grade point average of 3.55 and ranked 20th in a class of 100 and another school reported that a student had a grade point average of 3.55 and ranked 75th out of a class of 100, everyone would have a more accurate understanding than if only the grade point averages were given.

A single table relating class rank to grade point average would serve the same purpose. A sample table, containing only hypothetical data, is in Figure 8.1. Comparing the grade point averages in the first column with those that are in parentheses, it is clear that grade standards are different at the two schools (assuming there are no differences in the learners). This type of information would go a long way toward combatting grade inflation and would give more realistic impressions about the achievement of learners.

Writing Reference Letters

Writing reference letters is another important way of reporting on the performance of learners. Adult educators write reference letters for many purposes. Probably the primary purpose is to provide information about their current and former learners to potential employers. They also write reference letters regarding learners who are applying to educational programs and learners who are participating in programs required of them by agencies such as the courts and departments of social services. Regardless of the specific reason for writing a reference letter, the guidelines for composing them are pretty much the same. Therefore, in order to simplify the presentation of those guidelines, this section is focused on writing reference letters for people who are applicants for employment.

The following guidelines are offered with a significant proviso. Readers should consult with their colleagues to ascertain

percentage of graduates	having GPAs higher than
25	3.5 (3.2)
50	3.3 (3.0)
75	3.0 (2.5)*

* GPAs in parenthesis are for school two

Figure 8.1 Percentile Ranks and Corresponding Grade Point Averages for Recent Graduates of Two Hypothetical Schools

the common practices for writing reference letters in their locales and think very seriously about the ramifications of doing anything contrary to those practices.

- Write reference letters only after receiving a written request for such a letter and limit the content of the letter to the information that was requested. Collaborate with the applicant in deciding what he or she wishes you to address in the letter. Be sure to discuss the advantages and disadvantages of waiving the right of access to the letter and state the applicant's decision in the letter. Also determine whether or not the applicant wants you to engage in phone calls or other communications that could function as reference letters.
- Write reference letters only after checking that you have adequate objective information to comment meaningfully and conveying to the applicant the nature of the letter you will write. Explain the guidelines (listed below) that you will follow. Stress that the letter will be descriptive rather than evaluative.
- Request a copy of the applicant's resume and a description of the position the applicant is pursuing.
- Base reference letters on valid assessment information that you have recorded and preserved. Attendance tallies, test scores, and portfolios of authentic assessments are examples. In addition, include multiple sources of information on a given issue. For example, in addressing the attitude of an applicant toward work, report on attendance, promptness, proportion

of work completed on time, etc. Stress factual information and offer interpretations of that information only when they are fully supported by objective information. It cannot be said that an applicant who completed both of two assignments on time "completes all work on time," nor can it be said that someone who completed only one of two assignments on time "has difficulty completing work on time." Both of these interpretations go beyond what is justified by the data.

- Resist pressures to write overly glowing reference letters. These pressures can be very powerful. For example, educators would feel considerable pressure if an administrator in a workforce preparation program reminded them of the importance of placing graduates in jobs in order to ensure continued funding of the program and cautioned them against putting applicants at a disadvantage by writing lukewarm reference letters. Similarly, educators feel pressure when applicants express a need for a job to pay their bills, support their families, and so forth. In the face of these or similar pressures, educators are likely to lose sight of their obligations to those potential employers and to the other applicants for the job and write overly glowing references for their learners.

- Write reference letters conscientiously because, like grades, reference letters can significantly affect the lives of applicants. Educators should not tell learners to write their own letters and then sign those letters as if they reflected the educators' judgments. Nor should they send a stock letter of reference that they alter minimally, if at all, for whomever requests one.

- Begin by stating that the letter was written at the request of the applicant. Also state that it is completely confidential and should not be shared with anyone who is not directly involved in making the decision about the applicant. If the applicant waived access to the letter, state that the letter should not be revealed to the applicant.

- State your policy of providing only factual information in reference letters as the best way to be fair to all concerned. Explain that your objective tone should not be interpreted to mean a lack of enthusiasm for the applicant or as anything other than an attempt to follow your policy.

- State whether you are writing a general letter of the "To Whom It May Concern" variety or a letter pertaining to an application for a particular job, or other purpose.
- State your qualifications for writing the letter. Your qualifications include your knowledge of the job the applicant is applying for as well as your knowledge of the applicant. They also include the length of time you have known the applicant and the nature of your relationship to the applicant. For example, you might be an educator, supervisor, colleague, and/or friend. Finally, specify the nature and the extent of your opportunities to assess the applicant's skills and qualities.
- Report all the relevant information about the applicant that you can document. Although you need to make judgments about what is relevant on a case-by case-basis, keep in mind that employers are typically interested in attitudes toward work, technical skills, oral and written communication, and group and interpersonal skills (Kleman and Wonder, 1986). Recognize that it is deceptive to report the positive information and withhold the negative information regarding an applicant.
- Report relevant information as you initially recorded the information. For example, "The information I have regarding his/her skills is based on the work he/she did on the major project in our program. A description of the project is enclosed. I rated the project using the enclosed rubric. His/her score was . . . " Report attendance records, test scores, and so forth in similar fashion. Normally, reference letters do not include comments from third parties. However, peer assessments of the sort described in Chapter 7 regarding performance in cooperative groups can be summarized and included.
- If it is necessary to rank an applicant in comparison to other learners, do so only if you can document the ranking. For example, if you state that a applicant is average, you should have not just a test score, but a full array of assessment data to buttress your conclusion. It is often appropriate to give the reader of the letter some help in interpreting the rankings. For example, there is quite a difference between saying, "She was an average student." and saying, "She was an average student.

Our records show that 90% of our students are successfully employed in the area of their training one year after they graduate so she should be considered well qualified in her area." Some people would latch onto the phrase average student in the former statement and conclude that as an average student she would not make a good worker. However, most people readily grasp the full picture when it is explained to them as it is in the latter statement.

- Refrain from offering personal opinions or speculations, and when you cannot refrain, be sure to label as such any comments that are personal opinions or speculations. On the other hand, it may be worthwhile to include a statement to indicate that you have no reservations about the applicant when you can make the statement in honesty because such statements clear away unfounded doubts about an applicant.
- Offer to engage in follow-up telephone conversations to clarify the contents of the letter and answer questions about the applicant if the applicant has given you permission to do so. Employers typically consider phone conversations to be more valid that letters so be prepared to receive follow-up calls and be sure to follow the guidelines for writing reference letters during those calls.
- Revise the letter so that it contains your best writing. A poorly written letter has the potential to reflect unfairly on the applicant.
- Release the letter only to the persons or agencies the learner designates.
- Avoid engaging in phone call or other communications for the purpose of serving as a reference unless the applicant has given you permission to do so even when potential employers initiate them.
- Never reveal anything about the applicant's race, color, national origin, age, religion, disability, health, sex, sexual orientation, family responsibilities, or marital status. To do so is an unwarranted invasion of privacy, and could result in a lawsuit. In general, refrain from revealing anything about the applicant except information regarding attitudes toward work, technical skills, oral and written communication, and group and interpersonal skills.

Academic Misconduct

Academic misconduct, sometimes called cheating, is a long-standing and growing concern among educators who give grades, certify competence, or make recommendations based upon educational assessment. It can take many forms—often it refers to either giving or receiving help in answering questions on an exam. It also includes having advance copies of the exam, and using aids such as fact sheets during closed-book exams. However, academic misconduct is not confined to exams. It also includes falsifying information as someone might do in "making up" or changing data that was to be gathered in a science experiment. One of the most problematic types of academic misconduct is plagiarism, which can be defined as offering another's products, words, and/or ideas as one's own as one might do in a written report.

As society has grown more litigious, there has been a growing need for institutions to develop policies regarding academic misconduct. These policies usually have two goals: One is to prevent the occurrence of misconduct and the second is to instill a sense of integrity in learners so that they will refrain from misconduct even if they thought they would not be detected. An institutional policy should explain several matters:

- the nature of academic misconduct
- the reasons it is considered a serious offense
- the responsibilities of the learners for reporting misconduct that they observe
- guidelines for educators in detecting, gathering evidence about, and reporting misconduct
- due process for assessing reports of misconduct
- penalties when reports are upheld

With the help of institutional policies, individual educators can and should address the problem of academic misconduct with their learners. They should distribute and discuss all institutional policies with learners. Educators who have not done so in the past will probably be surprised to hear about the many ways learners understand and misunderstand the concept. Plagiarism especially should be discussed because it becomes more of an issue as learners attempt the sorts of independent work associated with adult education.

Where there is no institutional policy, educators should explain and develop their own policies to address the same matters outlined above. They should clear their policies with supervisors to avoid conflicts with other institutional policies and to avoid problems in implementing what they have developed. For example, some educators have been surprised to learn that seeing someone cheat on a test is insufficient evidence of cheating; observations must be substantiated by other evidence such as an admission or a cheat sheet in order to be sustained in a legal or due process action.

Having provided examples of what constitutes academic misconduct, educators should take precautions not to tempt learners. For example, they should monitor exams, avoid reusing entire exams or even large portions of exams, and schedule exams in large rooms where learners are spread out. Learners may become tempted to plagiarize when they are facing deadlines they believe they cannot meet. Educators can help in this regard by holding conferences with learners well before the deadlines. In the conferences the educator can assess the progress learners are making on their projects, help shape the project so that submitting some other person's work will not occur, keep the learners on schedule, and engender sufficient confidence in their work that learners are relieved of the temptation.

MULTICULTURALISM AND DIVERSITY

Whereas the aforementioned concerns for achieving coherence in assessment activities within institutions have arisen from a growing awareness of assessment principles within the community of educators, concerns for accommodating multiculturalism and diversity have emerged from the changing demographics of American learners. From an assessment standpoint, the goal is to celebrate diversity among learners without overestimating, underestimating, or otherwise misperceiving the achievement of any individual.

The difficulties come from at least two sources. One is primarily cognitive. Learners who are familiar with certain content areas have an advantage in solving problems and organizing material in those areas. Similarly, lack of familiarity or facility with the language in which a test is written is a disadvantage in solving problems and organizing material covered on the test.

The second is more motivational. Assessment practices, like all educational practices, must encourage learners. One of the important ways of encouraging learners from different cultural groups is to recognize the achievements of people who share their cultures. Therefore, it has become an axiom that all cultural groups should be portrayed in equally diverse, powerful, competent, and responsible positions in all assessment activities. In this context, cultural groups are defined in terms of race, ethnicity, religion, gender, national origin, sexual orientation, geographical region, age, social class, disability, occupation, marital status, and similar dimensions. Portrayal refers to the implicit and explicit ways in which the groups are discussed. For example, if the Plebeians are said to have "won rights" from the Patricians in ancient Rome, and the colonists are said to have "won independence" from England, but women were "granted the vote," then women have been portrayed as a group lacking in power and competence. Equity in assessment requires that educators work to abolish negativity and present positive portraits of all people in all their dimensions. It is a significant challenge considering the diversity of people and the possibilities of appearing excessively politically correct, but it is a challenge worth accepting.

Cultural difference issues arise at many points in the assessment process. Some of the major problems are discussed below.

Bias in Language

One of the more obvious types of bias is in language, particularly sexist language. Several organizations have recently published guidelines for nonsexist language. *Bias Issues in Test Development* (National Evaluation Systems, Inc., 1991) and *Publication Manual of the American Psychological Association* (American Psychological Association, 1994) are particularly helpful. One of the more general guidelines is to avoid statements in which one group is used as an implicit standard for one or more other groups. One of the more common and easily avoided violations of this guideline is the convention, in English, of using a masculine pronoun to refer to men and women. For example, "Each graduate will walk across the stage to receive his diploma," can be rephrased as "All graduates will walk across the stage to receive their diplomas." A very different type of violation of this same guideline occurs in the title, *The Ascent of Man*. It could be considered a case of sexist language because it uses the word man to refer to women as well as men. It may be doubly unfortunate because it seems to suggest that men, not women, represent the evolutionary achievement.

A second type of bias in language is found in the terms used to refer to minority groups. Names are clearly important to people, and we show respect by calling people by the names they prefer and recognizing that the names preferred by groups will change as peoples' perceptions of themselves change. Therefore, educators have a responsibility to keep themselves aware of the names that are preferred at a given point in time and use those preferred names. Otherwise, they at least give the appearance of being unwilling to consider the sensitivities of others.

People with disabilities have recommended "person first" language as a way of minimizing a third type of bias in language. The idea is to emphasize an individual's humanity and ability over his or her disability by using the word *person* first and mentioning the disability second. Person with a disability is preferable to a disabled person; person with epilepsy is preferable to epileptic; and lawyer with a disability is preferable to disabled lawyer. Although there may be times when it is better to depart from the "person first" language, the concept of emphasizing humanity over individual characteristics would seem to be a useful guide.

Bias in Content

Bias in language and bias in content sometimes seem to merge as they do for people who speak English as a second language. They may spend so much time trying to understand test questions that they have little time left to answer the questions based on knowledge of content. The bias in assessment caused by language differences is relatively public for all to see, but it is also difficult to mitigate. Allowing learners to use dictionaries and to take extra time are probably the most feasible tactics.

There are more subtle problems experienced by people who have come to the United States from non-English-speaking countries. They have difficulty—lack of familiarity—with particular English vocabulary domains including cooking, transportation, sports, musical instruments, and holidays. In addition, they often have limited familiarity with people, places, and events in American history. "When these terms and events are included in item stems, we are testing not only the intended topic but also students' understanding of American vocabulary and culture" (Eggen & Kauchak, 1994).

Clearly, it is helpful for educators to be aware of how different groups are likely to be disadvantaged in particular content areas in order to avoid predictable problems. However, it may be more important to address the issue of item bias by discussing it openly with all learners. It would be helpful to give illustrations of how learners might be disadvantaged on particular items and what they could do about it. For example, they could be told to ask for clarification of items they don't understand and that the educator will explain terms when appropriate. The educator could give examples of questions that could be answered and examples of questions that could not be answered. A pair of such examples follow: A test to determine how well a learner could reason by analogy contained the following item: baking : cooking :: car : a. truck; b. vehicle; c. train; d. food. If a learner asked, "What is baking?" the educator could give a factual explanation. Should the learner ask, "What is the difference between baking and cooking?" the educator would say that he or she could explain baking and cooking, but not the differences because recognizing the difference was part of what was being tested. Welcoming questions and responding politely whether with an answer or an explanation that an answer cannot be given is key.

There are additional considerations. When explanations are given, people have a tendency to act as if they understand even when they don't. The less confident the person the more likely he or she is to feign understanding. Cheng (cited by Eggen & Kauchak, 1994) has reported that Asian students are known to feign understanding as a sign of courtesy. Considering this possibility, the educator who gives an explanation of a term on a test would do well to ask something like: "Let's make sure I explained everything properly. Please, use your own words to tell me what I said."

A less obvious type of problem is caused when educators place test items within real-life contexts. Although connecting test items to real-life contexts is often desirable, as the following example reveals, it can also be a source of bias. The following percentage problem (Eggen & Kauchak, 1994) is given to a diverse group:

> John Carey is presently batting .300 after one hundred trips to the plate. In his next three times at bat, he gets a single, double, and home run. What is his batting average now? Word problems using content that not all . . . can be expected to know (e.g., how batting averages [are] computed and do doubles and home runs count more than singles?) can unfairly penalize females or minorities who don't have prerequisite background knowledge. Math word problems can also be biased if [learners] miss the problem because of limited reading skills rather than lack of conceptual or computational skills in math. (p. 701)

A closely related but frequently overlooked idea is that the more familiarity individuals have with a content area, the more readily they will be able to process information within that content area. If a mathematics instructor presents word problems that are couched in terms of sports, learners who know about the sports will have an advantage compared to learners who do not know much about sports, but that is not all. Two boys of comparable achievement who both understand the procedures for computing batting averages might perform quite differently on the batting average problem. If one boy follows batting averages, and computes them for his Little League team, he is likely to do better than a boy who is less interested in baseball and could care less about them. If problems are couched in terms of finances, recipes, carpentry, tailoring, auto mechanics, or gardening, people with expertise in those areas will be advantaged. Ultimately, educators must choose between eliminating the real-life contexts from tests or trying to use such a large variety of material that they advantage all people equally.

Content bias can occur in the selection of material that appears on a test. The people whose names are mentioned in examples, and whose achievements are singled out for praise, become designated as the admirable ones. Therefore, educators must mention members of all groups otherwise they tacitly demean those groups that are not mentioned. Although this type of content bias is easy to understand in principle, it is not always easy to know what steps to take in order to mitigate the problem. For example, in a mathematics course where many word problems are assigned, what percentage of the main characters should have names suggesting membership in each demographic group in the country? in the state? in the learners who will take the test?

It should be obvious that no educator is ever going to know how to deal with all the possible occurrences of cultural bias. Therefore, educators need to review tests with colleagues and learners to get a thorough understanding of how cultural differences are influencing their learners. In fact, each time a test is assessed, educators should check for cultural bias. The more interest educators display in accommodating the cultures of diverse populations, the more forthcoming the learners will be, and the more successful the learning programs.

Bias in Test Procedures

Eggen and Kauchak (1994) remind us that the very process of structured individual paper and pencil testing is incompatible with some cultures because it is more competitive than cooperative. The extreme case is when learners are given a paper and pencil test that is graded on a curve. For all of its technical merit, the competitive feature is contrary to certain cultures and counterproductive for the learners. Eggen and Kauchak (1994) mention that this is particularly true of African American and Native American learners. When learners come from cultures where testing is alien, the measures mentioned in Chapter 3 for reducing test anxiety are especially needed.

Timed tests exacerbate the problems of competitive testing. They are also thought to be especially harmful to older learners who may be processing information more slowly or having trouble with vision. These two difficulties may be acute with both objective and essay tests. So it is worth noting that multiple-choice tests may be particularly appropriate for older adults who are beginning to have problems recalling material stored in memory, but have fewer problems selecting a correct answer when it is printed out for them.

Testing learners in a language other than their first language may constitute a serious bias in test procedures. Unfortunately, very few educators have the capacity to conduct informal assessments in more than one language. Therefore, it is necessary to find ways of minimizing the effect of language differences. As mentioned above, two of the simplest adjustments involve having learners use dictionaries during tests and taking additional time to complete tests. These adjustments and others mentioned below in the section on learners with disabilities are not to be confused with giving extra help to selected learners. They are merely ways of giving all learners equal opportunity to demonstrate their achievements. Indeed, equal opportunity is the concept that guides all decisions about when to alter test procedures for individual learners.

As vexing as these problems with test procedures are, it may be wise to look to portfolios as a sound method to avoid all the sources of test bias mentioned above.

Learners with Disabilities

Multiculturalism has heightened awareness that educational assessment is meant to determine what a person has accomplished in terms of specified learning objectives and that barriers to successful performance in the form of irrelevant test features should be detected and eliminated. Recently educators have become more aware of their responsibilities for addressing these barriers as they affect persons with disabilities. They have also found that their responsibilities are often very easy to discharge. Frequently, no more is required than a single adjustment for a single learner within a group. For example, a person with a learning disability in spelling could be accommodated by deciding that spelling errors will not lower his or her grade on essay and short answer test questions.

Detecting barriers to successful test performance can be more demanding than eliminating them. The first step in detection is to extend, at the beginning of a learning program, an invitation to consult with anyone who might need special testing accommodations. Placing such an invitation in a course syllabus or other handout at the beginning of a learning program not only delivers the message to those who may need it, but demonstrates the approachability of the educator to all the learners.

Adult educators should not simply rely on their learners to identify themselves because many times adult learners are reluctant to do so. They may be trying to compensate for their disabilities and want to test their progress in doing so. They may fear being stigmatized. They may not even know they have an actual disability. Therefore, educators need to be constantly alert for signs of a disability. Certain types of disability such as blindness and motor problems are more readily recognized than others such as attention deficits. In addition, there may be a tendency to observe that a learner has a disability and fail to consider the possibility that he or she might have a second one.

It is beyond the scope of this book to detail the procedures for screening for the presence of a disability. In general, educators need to note the situations where learners perform relatively well and relatively poorly. When the differences between the good and the poor performances become large and predictable, the possibility exists that a disability is contributing to the poor performances. Asking the learner if he or she has noticed the same pattern of success and failures is an appropriate first step, but suggesting that a disability is present is not acceptable. If the learner agrees that he or she does have a history of poor performance in a particular circumstance, it would be appropriate to ask about ways to address the problem and to refer the learner to an expert in helping people with persistent learning problems.

It is important to keep in mind that using the term disability creates a misleading sense that disabilities are all or nothing occurrences. In fact, there is every level of impairment in every sphere of functioning. One person might have particularly acute hearing, another might be unable to hear speech under ideal circumstances and is recognized as having a hearing impairment. A third might have difficulty hearing only in certain circumstances such as when there is background noise. Whereas the first person mentioned needs no accommodations, and the second person may bring documentation of a disability complete with recommendations for accommodations, the third person deserves accommodations as the need arises, but he or she may be easily overlooked.

Types of Disabilities and Accommodations

The following discussion of disabilities might help educators in their efforts to recognize disabilities and adapt assessments accordingly. The suggested accommodations are not meant to be prescriptive or exhaustive, but illustrative of the types of accommodations that educators would make routinely.

Sensory Impairments

From the standpoint of informal assessment, a hearing impairment is a particular problem when directions for taking a test are given. It may cause a learner to miss out on the formal instructions to a group of learners as well as the questions other learners ask about the test and the answers they receive. Providing preferred seating, writing out instructions, repeating questions asked by others, and facing the person(s) to facilitate lip reading are the most obvious adaptations.

Vision impairment is a major barrier to successful performance on traditional tests. It can interfere with reading the tests, and it can interfere with recording answers on both computer scan sheets and lined paper. Accommodations could be as low tech as having a helper read the test and record answers. They could be as high tech as using machine readers.

Motor Impairments

Motor impairments are disabilities that affect movement including small muscle movement involved in writing and speaking. Adaptations include ready access to assessment facilities with proctors to aid in producing and recording responses. Often it may be helpful to have learners use word processors to record their responses, but allowing extra time may be the simplest and most effective adaptation.

Emotional Impairments

Emotional impairments come in many forms and levels of severity. It seems likely that test anxiety may be the most common form. When it is mild, it may actually improve test performance, but at higher levels it can be incapacitating. The procedures for reducing test anxiety mentioned in Chapter 3 might be sufficient for some learners, but for others, educators can recommend treatment from a counseling center and/or alter the assessment format. Alterations might include, assigning a term paper or take-home examination to measure the same learning objectives. To avoid possible resentments among other learners, educators should alter the format for all the learners or only for individuals who have some documentation that they suffer unusual test anxiety.

Depression appears to be a marked contrast to anxiety. It drains a learner of the desire to do well and the energy to produce, to get to class and even to concentrate. It can be either long- or short-term, and it can be feigned. Long-term depression should be treated by a mental health professional and can be documented. Whenever depression is so documented, the educator can request consultation with the mental health professional regarding adaptations to the assessment process. On the other hand, acute short-term depression cannot be so readily documented. An educator who is presented with a request to allow a learner to delay taking a test until a source of depression is relieved can be decidedly uncertain about what to do. In such situations it is helpful to recall that the primary reason for assessing learning is to enhance learning. It is not to punish, or hold people accountable, or teach personal responsibility. In the absence of clear information to the contrary, it would seem appropriate to lean toward accommodating the learner.

Specific Learning Disabilities

A specific learning disability is a marked difficulty in a particular academic domain despite average or even above average intelligence. Like the other disabilities, specific learning disabilities must be diagnosed by professionals. What makes them different is that they can appear to be quite mysterious to someone who has not been educated about them. The following example illustrates the sometimes baffling quality of specific learning disabilities. A man was referred for an evaluation of his persistent problems in reading. He performed in the average range on an intelligence test, and in conversation he was bright and personable. Toward the end of the evaluation he was asked to pronounce words from a printed list. At one point, he paused over a word, and said, "It's rot with t in front of it, but I can't pronounce it." From this comment, it seems clear that the man has the ability and is making an effort to employ his analytical skills, but he has marked difficulty in this one area of transferring the written word to the spoken word. One can imagine the frustration he feels and the frustration that probably has been vented on him by parents, teachers, colleagues, and others.

It is easy to see how this specific disability can interfere with learning and assessment in many ways. Readers interested in the recent advances in educating adult learners with specific learning disabilities may wish to consult Jordan (1996). For the moment, the focus is on assessment issues and the challenge to the educator to assess a particular individual's achievement without letting the disability depress his or her score. One possibility is to make some of the same adaptations that are made for a person with a vision impairment while ensuring that he is making the most of whatever academic support services are available to him.

People may have comparable difficulties in virtually any of the basic aspects of transmitting information. Reading seems to be the most common area of learning disabilities, but many educators will have learners with disabilities in areas such as spelling, calculating, sequencing, and memorizing. Adaptations for learners with specific learning disabilities are quite varied and include virtually all the adaptations mentioned in regard to other types of disabilities. For example, a person who has specific difficulty in writing may need the same adaptations as a person with a motor problem. Very often, learners with specific learning disabilities may profit by taking examinations in a private room or in a room that is otherwise free of distractions.

Health-Related Disabilities

The health-related disabilities are a broad range of problems that cause people chronic pain or cause them to take medications that affect their attention and learning. Adaptations for assessment often include provisions to make people physically comfortable and are among the most individual adaptations. The disabilities may also be progressive so an educator may want to check with learners to see if adaptations made in the past continue to be appropriate.

Generally it is fairly easy to accommodate adult learners with disabilities because they are typically interested in being independent and providing their own strategies, aids, and auxiliary devices. When experts in dealing with accommodating learner needs are available, they should be consulted regularly. Whether or not such an expert is available, it is desirable to discuss means of adapting assessment activities directly with the learners. Even learners with similar disabilities will sometimes need different accommodations, and choosing those accommodations with their input not only ensures a better fit to their needs, but it empowers them in the process of overcoming the disability.

It is beyond the scope of this book to address the legal aspects of assessing learners with disabilities. The principle of ensuring equal opportunities for learners with disabilities has been incorporated into law for some time. It has been strengthened in the Americans with Disabilities Act of 1990. Exactly how that latest law applies to the different adult education settings is still being worked out. In the meantime, expressed willingness to accommodate will be and may always be the single best policy.

This section illustrates the large number of responsibilities an educator assumes in working in a diverse multicultural environment. One of the best ways of fulfilling those responsibilities is to consult regularly with a circle of colleagues who themselves constitute a multicultural and diverse group. The consultations should include, but should not be limited to, assessment issues. They might even serve as the basis for a program of professional growth as outlined in the next section.

PROFESSIONAL DEVELOPMENT

Since educational assessment is conducted primarily in order to improve learning, educators want to assess all aspects of their learning programs, including that very influential factor—their own performance. A number of techniques exist for this purpose. The Small Group Instructional Diagnosis (SGID), teaching portfolios, and holistic assessments, all mentioned in earlier chapters, have direct applications to assessing educator performance and pointing the way to professional growth. Many institutions as well as individual educators commonly use end-of-course evaluation questionnaires completed by learners as a means of assessing performance in order to improve teaching and learning.

Peer Support

Perhaps the single most effective procedure for promoting professional growth is a peer support and assessment program

(Moran, Howe, & Wild, 1995). The core of such a program is an agreement between two or more educators to hold regular conferences to assess one another's performance for the sole purpose of helping one another become more effective in their professional activities.

The agreements can take whatever form the educators choose. Since everyone, educators included, is wary of being assessed, a good way to start out is by assessing whatever is least threatening. Often that means assessing learning materials that one another are developing. These might be plans for a workshop, overhead slides, or objective examinations. As trust and expertise develop, the peers might assess one another's teaching portfolios and ultimately conduct SGID with each other's classes.

The review is followed by a conference conducted as portfolio assessment conferences where one educator is the learner and the other the facilitator. On another occasion the roles are reversed. These peer support arrangements can be used to examine virtually every aspect of practice. They also offer a social dimension to the educator's professional life. Perhaps most important, they constitute a public commitment to professional growth that promotes effort and ultimately enhances practice.

Readers might consult Moran (2001) for a comprehensive account of professional development practices for teachers of adults.

ETHICAL CONCERNS

Looking back at the topics covered in this chapter and the earlier chapters it seems clear that informal educational assessment can have a very great impact on the lives of learners. When it is done properly, it leads to improved learning and in turn to opportunities for vocational advancement and personal happiness. When it is done improperly, it can be discouraging for learners and may close off opportunities for them. Therefore, educators have a significant responsibility to conduct informal assessment ethically. However, there are surprisingly few guidelines regarding the ethical conduct of educational assessment.

Those that do exist were developed by the American Psychological Association (1985) and pertain primarily to standardized testing and not to informal assessment. The situation is complicated by the fact that educators do not routinely receive training in this important aspect of their profession, and by the fact that assessment practices continually change so that an educator will never be fully trained in assessment practices.

Partly as an attempt to open a discussion of ethical concerns in informal assessment, and partly to summarize the content of this book, the following principles for ethical informal assessment are offered as the closing passage. They are based on the belief that any slackening from what one knows to be the highest standards of assessment practice is a disservice to the learners and might be considered unethical.

- Observe the established principles of instrument construction.
- Use a variety of assessment techniques.
- Ensure that all assessment activities are fair to all learners involved.
- Base interpretations about each learner's educational achievement on information from as many relevant sources as possible.
- Reference all interpretations of assessment data to norms and criteria.
- Make assessment interpretations encouraging to learners.
- Keep assessment data and interpretations confidential.
- Adopt expertise in assessment as a goal in plans for professional development.
- Discuss problematic situations within a peer support or mentor relationship.
- Maintain a primary focus on improving learning.

SUMMARY

The first seven chapters have focused on knowledge and skills that enable an individual educator to conduct assessment in ways that improve the learning of those they serve. This last chapter demonstrates the need for educators to cooperate in conducting informal assessment. Collaborating to develop guidelines for consistent assessment practices, consulting on multicultural and diversity issues, supporting one another's professional growth, and sharing ethical concerns are all important ways for educators to pool their individual competencies to achieve quality programs of informal assessment.

REFERENCES

American Psychological Association. (1985). *Standards for educational and psychological testing.* Washington, DC: Author.

American Psychological Association. (1994). *Publication manual of the American Psychological Association* (4th ed.). Washington, DC: Author.

Angelo, T. A., & Cross, K. P. (1993). *Classroom assessment techniques: A handbook for college teachers.* San Francisco: Jossey-Bass.

Bloom, B. S., Engelhart, M. D., Furst, E. J., Hill, W. H., & Krathwohl, D. R. (1956). *Taxonomy of educational objectives: Handbook I. Cognitive domain.* New York: D. McKay.

Brookfield, S. (1990). *The skillful teacher.* San Francisco: Jossey-Bass.

Coffman, S. J. (1991). Improving your teaching through small group diagnosis. *College Teaching, 39,* 80–82.

Dean, G. J. (1994). *Designing instruction for adult learners.* Malabar, FL: Krieger.

Diamond, N. (1988). SGID: Tapping student perceptions of teaching. In E. C. Wadsworth (Ed.), *Professional and organizational development in higher education: A handbook for new practitioners* (pp. 89–93). Stillwater, OK: New Forums Press.

Eggen, P., & Kauchak, D. (1994). *Educational psychology.* Toronto: Maxwell Macmillan Canada.

Foos, P., & Fisher, R. (1988). Using tests as learning opportunities. *Journal of Educational Psychology, 80,* 179–183.

Gronlund, N., & Linn, R. (1990). *Measurement and evaluation in teaching.* New York: Macmillan.

Grow, G. (1991). Teaching learners to be self-directed. *Adult Education Quarterly, 41,* 125–149.

Harris, B. (1989). *In-service education for staff development.* Boston: Allyn and Bacon.

Hart, D. (1994). *Authentic assessment.* New York: Addison-Wesley.

Johnson, D. W., Johnson, R. T., and Smith, K. A. (1998). Co-operative learning returns to college. *Change, 30,* 27–35.

Jordan, D. R. (1996). *Teaching adults with learning disabilities.* Malabar, FL: Krieger.

Kirkpatrick, D. L. (1998). *Evaluating training programs: The four levels.* (2nd ed.). San Francisco: Berrett-Koehler.

Kleman, K. S., and Wonder, B. D. (1986). Reference information: What do employers prefer? *Journal of career planning and employment, 46,* 57–60.

Knowles, M. (1980). *The modern practice of adult education.* New York: Cambridge.

Knowles, M. (1986). *Using learning contracts.* San Francisco: Jossey-Bass.

Long, H. B. (1990, October). *Holistic evaluation.* Paper presented at the meeting of the American Association for Adult and Continuing Education, Salt Lake City, UT.

Mezirow, J. (1991). *Transformational dimensions of adult learning.* San Francisco: Jossey-Bass.

Moran, J. J. (1991). Promoting cognitive development through adult education. *Education, 112,* 186–194.

Moran, J. J. (2001). *Collaborative professional development for teachers of adults.* Malabar, FL: Krieger.

Moran, J. J., Howe, F. C., & Wild, L. A. (1995, November). *Facilitating professional development through peer support.* Paper presented at the meeting of the American Association for Adult and Continuing Education, Kansas City, MO.

Murray, J. P. (1995). The teaching portfolio: A tool for department chairpersons to create a climate of teaching excellence. *Innovative Higher Education, 19,* 163–175.

National Evaluation Systems, Inc. (1991). *Bias issues in test development.* Amherst, MA.: Author.

Simpson, G. W. (1995). Cooperative learning with adults: Don't assume anything. *Adult Learning, 6*(4), 10–11.

Sternberger, C. (1995). Adult learning strategies. *Adult Learning, 6,* 12–13.

Stiggins, R. J. (1994). *Student-centered classroom assessment.* New York: Merrill.

Trice, A.D. (2000). *A handbook of classroom assessment.* New York: Addison Wesley Longman, Inc.

Vella, J., Berardinelli, P., and Burrow, J. (1998). *How do they know they know?* San Francisco: Jossey-Bass.

Wislock, R. F. (1993). What are perceptual modalities and how do they contribute to learning? In D. D. Flannery (Ed.), *Applying cognitive learning theory to adult learning* (pp. 5–13). New Directions for Adult and Continuing Education, no. 59. San Francisco: Jossey-Bass.

INDEX